THE ORIGINS AND PSYCHODYNAMICS

OF CREATIVITY

THE
ORIGINS AND
PSYCHODYNAMICS
OF CREATIVITY

A Psychoanalytic Perspective

Jerome D. Oremland, M.D.

INTERNATIONAL UNIVERSITIES PRESS, INC.
Madison • Connecticut

 # 35364817

Copyright © 1997, International Universities Press, Inc.

INTERNATIONAL UNIVERSITIES PRESS and International Universities Press, Inc. (& design)® are registered trademarks of International Universities Press, Inc.

Library of Congress Cataloging-in-Publication Data

Oremland, Jerome D.
    The origins and psychodynamics of creativity : a psychoanalytic perspective / Jerome D. Oremland.
      p.   cm.
    Includes bibliographical references and index.
    ISBN 0-8236-3905-3
    1. Creative ability. 2. Dream interpretation. 3. Psychoanalysis and art. I. Title.
BF408.074 1997
153.3'5—dc20
        96-43194
        CIP

Manufactured in the United States of America

To and for Evie

Contents

Illustrations   ix
Preface   xi
Introduction   xiii
1. Meaning in Art and Psychoanalysis   1
2. The Dream, Art, and Psychoanalysis   23
3. Dream Interpretation and Art Appreciation   35
4. Talent and Creativity   51
5. Creativity and Relatedness   83
6. Creativity and Sexuality   109
7. Responses   123
   A Painter Responds   123
   A Director Responds   131
   A Sculptor Responds   140
   A Businessman Responds   151
   The Author Responds   160
   References   167
   Index   175

Illustrations

Figure 1. *Judith,* Francesco Maffei 7

Figure 2. *St. John,* Leonardo da Vinci 10

Figure 3. *St. Anne and Two Others,* Leonardo da Vinci 11

Figure 4. *Mona Lisa,* Leonardo da Vinci 12

Figure 5. *Cartoon for Madonna with St. John and St. Anne,* Leonardo da Vinci 13

Figure 6. *Florentine pietà,* Michelangelo 15

Figure 7. *Madonna with St. Anne,* Michelangelo 16

Figure 8. *St. Peter's pietà,* Michelangelo 17

Figure 9. *Rondanini pietà,* Michelangelo 19

Figure 10. *Moses,* Michelangelo 20

Figure 11. *Ardhanarisvara,* Chola Dynasty 112

Figure 12. *Leda and the Swan,* Michelangelo, (Bos Copy) 113

Figure 13. *Separation of Light from Darkness,* Michelangelo 114

Figure 14. *Sacrifice of Noah,* Michelangelo 115

Figure 15. *Ignudi,* Michelangelo 116

Figure 16. *Cosmos,* Aris Demetrios 143

Figure 17. *Portal Series I,* Aris Demetrios 148

Figure 18. *My Space,* Aris Demetrios 150

Figure 19. *Scaffolding Series I,* Aris Demetrios 152

Preface

This book, long in the making, could not have come into being without the help and encouragement of my wife, Evelyn K. Oremland, to whom it is dedicated. Even though many of the ideas were initiated in my writings about art and artists, increasingly I realized that I had hidden much of what I thought about creating and creative individuals in these discussions. I came to realize that it was the majesty and complexity of the subject that had kept me from directly addressing creativity, although I dared subtitle my book on the Sistine Ceiling *A Psychoanalytic Study of Creativity*.

The book rotates around a few hard-won themes. The density of the text, I hope, reflects the complexity of the subject and a dedication to never taking the easy path in explanation. The themes largely are derived from reading about artists, talking with artists, and looking at creative endeavors from a psychoanalytic perspective. Most of all, I am indebted to my psychoanalytic work with artists as the primary source of new ideas and a major way of confirming their validity.

Although the book rests heavily on an investigation of the plastic arts, the area of creativity I know best, slowly I came to appreciate what is meant by *the artist* irrespective of medium, field, or endeavor. In a related way, distinguishing talent from creativity expanded and in curious ways limited the scope of what I regard as art and the artist.

Central to the book is the emphasis on the rather obvious fact that the artist is primarily communicating. My contribution rests on my understanding of *with whom*. This emphasis shifted my thinking from the more usual psychoanalytic view of creativity as defensive to thinking of creativity as a form of relating, a kind of inner dialogue, and an integral part of humankind's enduring desire for continuity. Creation, be it issue or art, is part of the quest for immortality.

Another theme in the book that feels secure is the analogy between the created and creating and the dream and dreaming and the importance of differentiating ambiguity from condensation, as understood psychoanalytically. The investigation of the nature of the creation of the dream is among the most enduring of all psychoanalytic ideas. I am indebted to the psychoanalytic developmentalists for providing the link between the dream and dreaming, the created and creating and ontogeny, the development of the self, and relatedness.

Personal experience with art gave me consistent confidence in the importance of the human developmental universals to art. Without its relationship to universals, art could only be topical, time limited, and culture bound.

Although I value my psychoanalytic colleagues who have contributed in many ways to this volume, my indebtedness largely lies with my artist friends who have told me of their experiences and listened patiently to my cumbersome attempts to place their subjective reality into different perspectives. Although it is difficult individually to mark their contributions, I am especially grateful to the four respondents, individuals easily identified as being creative. Watching them, talking with them, reading their responses, and realizing how similar is their approach, despite their widely different fields of endeavor, gave me confidence in my underlying thesis: creative individuals are as different from others as they are like each other in the way they think.

Introduction

Freud's explorations of creativity are intrinsic to the origins of psychoanalysis. In letters to Wilhelm Fliess (1887–1902), widely regarded as the beginnings of psychoanalysis, conspicuous among Freud's speculations are thoughts about *Hamlet*. This initial exploration of the play, coupled with later exploration of the analogy between the dream and the created object, condensed a number of paradigms that have been pursued singularly by subsequent scholars, resulting in a large corpus that comprises the psychoanalytic explorations of creativity.

It is of note that Freud's early study of creativity centered on a work of art rather than on its creator or the process of creating. In the Fliess correspondence, Freud identified a latent theme in *Hamlet* (Shakespeare, 1600), which he held accounted for the enduring fascination with the play. Placing emphasis on Hamlet's inability to retaliate for his father's murder and the seduction of his mother by his uncle, Claudius, Freud posited that Hamlet at a level was psychically paralyzed by his identification with Claudius in that the uncle had done what Hamlet unconsciously wished to have done. Freud saw this dramatic enactment of oedipal triangulation as the organizing universal that gave the play profound meaning, crossing epoch and culture.

Freud developed his ideas regarding *Hamlet* more fully in chapter 4 of *The Interpretation of Dreams* (1900). There the play surprisingly becomes evidence for his view of the universality of the oedipal triangulation and the central place of oedipal considerations in the formation of neurotic symptoms, character

function, and in the establishment and continuation of genera-
tional and cultural institutions.

Freud's thesis on the play was refined in Ernest Jones' *Hamlet and Oedipus* (1949), which set the way for a cadre of essays
glorifying and condemning psychoanalytic exposition of art. The
psychoanalytic *Hamlet* literature was significantly advanced by
Kurt Eissler's *Discourse on Hamlet and "Hamlet"* (1971) and
the serious, thoughtful, sometimes bitter refutations of psychoanalytic studies of creativity (Prosser, 1971).

Beyond the specific criticism of psychoanalytic postulates
in general and of Freud's Shakespeare scholarship in particular,
a central paradigm endures: the evocative power in artistic masterpieces resides in their portraying human universals and developmental fundamentals, a position that has come under strong
attack from nearly all quarters studying artistic creation (Schapiro, 1956; Prosser, 1971; Hibbard, 1974; Tolnay, 1975; Steinberg, 1984).

It is noteworthy that Freud's study of *Hamlet* is not a psychopathological study, although it is frequently alleged to be.
Freud presents the drama of the play as an enactment of normative developmental imperatives, a proposal contrasting with studies of *Hamlet* as a depiction of psychopathology; as an example,
Hamlet as a portrayal of obsessive doubting and weakened con-
stitution (Goethe, 1795) and arrested development (Webster,
1948). While psychopathological studies of fictional characters
must be approached cautiously, such studies are not to be depreciated. It must be acknowledged that just as fiction has created
enduring and full "personalities," fiction has provided rich, re-
warding, and remarkably valid depictions of the phenomena and
origins of psychopathology.

Embedded in Freud's study of *Hamlet* is another paradigm,
which generally has eclipsed the psychoanalytic study of the
evocation of art. Using the biographical information at his dis-
posal, Freud noted that the writing of *Hamlet* followed closely
upon the death of Shakespeare's young son Hamnet and Shakespeare's father, John. Accurately sensing that the play overall is

an explication of death and that the play's characters can be read as allegories of the range of responses of human beings to death, Freud posited that writing the play was part of the mourning of John's and Hamnet's deaths (Oremland, 1983). In a nonspecific way Freud initiated the study of events, conscious and unconscious, past and present in the lives of creative individuals and how these events trigger, alter, modify, motivate, and find expressions in their creativity. In the study of *Hamlet*, Freud suggested a specific relation between personal events and creativity, that creative people may use their creativity as part of their bereavement in a manner parallel to mourning in ordinary individuals.[1] This view has at times mistakenly been seen as Freud's suggesting that personal losses produce creativity.

Psychoanalytic biographical study of creative individuals, which Freud called *pathography*, reached its apogee in his monograph on Leonardo da Vinci (Freud, 1910). In the Leonardo monograph Freud traced the possible relation of a childhood memory to important personality characteristics and specific representations in Leonardo's art. In the monograph are important prefigurings of a recognition of basic relationships between the art image and the dream image.

---

[1] As an aside, there is an unexplained inconsistency in Freud's writing on Shakespeare. Although he linked Shakespeare's writing of *Hamlet* to the death of Hamnet and John, we know that Freud had an extensive correspondence in which he held firm to the conviction that the plays were written by Edward de Vere, the Earl of Oxford, reasoning that the plays could not have been written by a man of Shakespeare's background or education (Freud, 1935).

Although this view reflects Freud's strong tendency to view creativity as constitutionally or hereditarily determined and his Victorian class prejudices, the inconsistency between his formal writing about the role of the deaths in the writing of *Hamlet* and his correspondence about who wrote the plays remains unexplained.

It also is of interest that Freud ignored *King John*, which was written closer to the time of these deaths than *Hamlet* and in which are some hauntingly memorable lines describing grief for a young son.

Constance: Grief fills the room up of my absent child,
Lies in his bed, walks up and down with me;
Puts on his pretty looks, repeats his words,
Remembers me of all his gracious parts,
Stuffs out his vacant garments with his form;
O Lord, my boy, . . . my life . . . my all the world!
[*King John*, Act III, Scene iv].

Although often criticized, pathographies have led to rich contributions to the study of art and artists. Refinements of the paradigm have demonstrated that the study of themes and forms in artwork fleshes out biographical studies of artists (J. Gedo, 1970; M. Gedo, 1980; Rose, 1980; Wilson, 1981). In these refinements art becomes the autobiography of artists' subjective experiences; Freud's pathography becomes depth biography, or better termed, in keeping with the psychoanalytic lexicon, *meta*-biography (M. Gedo, 1980; Oremland, 1989).[2] This *meta*-autobiographic view of art frees psychoanalytic studies from a psychopathological context. That is not to say that there is not usefulness in the study of psychopathology in creative individuals and its effect on their art, but such works as Peter Ostwald's (1985, 1991) studies of the psychopathology of Robert Schumann and Nijinski and Albert Lubin's (1976) study of Van Gogh are a different order of investigation.

These primary paradigms, the effects of the artist's personal experience on creativity and the relation of art to the expression of human universals as determined by developmental imperatives, when combined with Freud's studies of the formation of the dream, become his fundamental contributions to the psychoanalytic study of creativity. Striking by their absence are speculations regarding the origins of creativity and the psychodynamics of the creating process.

The purpose of this book is further to evaluate these psychoanalytic paradigms, to explore their strengths and weaknesses, and to augment the psychoanalytic study of art by presenting a psychoanalytic perspective on the origins and psychodynamics of creativity.

---

[2] Freud coined the term *metapsychology* for his study of an area of psychology. He attached the Greek prefix *meta*, beyond, to psychology to give the sense of studies transcending descriptive and experimental psychology. I employ the prefix *meta* with biography to give the sense of studies transcending the usual meaning of biography, writing about a life. I have in mind that art provides the meta-autobiography of the artist's subjective life of which the artist is only dimly aware or completely unaware, which when studied and interpreted can become metabiography (Oremland, 1989).

Meaning in Art and Psychoanalysis

The idea that personal experiences, conscious and unconscious, find disguised expression in the themes and forms of creative works, widely regarded as the primary paradigm of a psychoanalytic investigation of creativity, is closely related to the psychoanalytic view of meaning. The idea of meaning in psychoanalysis is derived from Freud's investigation of hysteria. This paradigm was to be elaborated into a full understanding of dreams, various enactments, and character traits. Early on, Freud (Breuer and Freud, 1893–1895) posited that physical symptoms when hysterical can be interpreted, that they have meaning. In an oversimplified way, interpretation of the symbolic meaning was early identified as the therapeutic effect of psychoanalysis and indelibly interrelated psychoanalysis, pathology, and treatment.

In the investigation of hysterical manifestations, Freud made two of his most generalizable observations, the return of the repressed and compromise formation. Freud surmised that the hysterical symptom represents, that it symbolizes, as a compromised expression, unacceptable wishes (concepts) and punishment concepts for the wishes. For example, blindness when hysterical is a physical expression of the forbidden desire to look and is a punishment for looking. This view of meaning was extended by the realization that the forbidden wish is related to early, dynamically forgotten (repressed), unacceptable experience subjectively enhanced and distorted by developmental and maturational imperatives and concerns. Typical of the psychoanalytic orientation, the manifestation (blindness) is seen as multilayered according to a depth metaphor.

In the depth metaphor, the surface is the precipitating event, an often unrecognized, sometimes seemingly insignificant current event "beneath" which resides symbolically related historical actualities. These actualities as intrapsychically retained are distorted in terms of developmental capacities. These are the psychic realities of the unconscious. The developmental circumstances that determine psychic realities are closely related to universal human maturational experiences. In a schematic way, all levels of meaning are economically interrelated by symbolic interconnections.

To illustrate this way of looking at things consider, continuing the blindness example, a young woman who while physically caring for her ill father suffers sudden blindness.[1] The precipitating event is the fear (desire) of seeing the father nude while caring for him. The punishment is hysterical blindness. The physical manifestation, blindness, is a composite, a compromised expression of the unacceptable wish (looking) and the punishment (blindness). The blindness expresses the wish to see, the punishment for wanting to see, and eliminates the temptation.

The unacceptable nature of the wish is related to a historical event. As a young child, she came upon the father in his bath. In the historical event, the father is visibly upset and scolds the little girl for not knocking before entering. Underlying this "accidental" entering the bathroom was the fearful guilt-laden wish to look, a developmental imperative related to infantile curiosities and sexuality. The guilt-laden desire to see the father naked intensified the little girl's reaction to the father's response.

---

[1] This simplified, fabricated, schematic example based on a composite of patient histories somewhat follows Joseph Breuer's first description of the treatment of a hysterical paralysis by psychoanalytic interpretations, published as "Fräulein Anna O" in *Studies on Hysteria* (Breuer and Freud, 1893–1895).

The "entering" and the scolding take on layers of significance. Although the surviving memory is only of accidental entrance and the scolding, the situation of caring for the ill father with the opportunity to satisfy old curiosities, reverberates to the repressed early experience. Viewed this way, the blindness has multiple meanings, adaptively (removes her from temptation), psychodynamically (the desire to look and the punishment for the desire), genetically (a childhood incident), and universally (oedipal wishes).

To summarize, psychoanalytic meaning, as illustrated by "understanding" the hysterical blindness, involves a multilayered appreciation of symbolic representations of topical (taking care of the father), personal (the childhood incident), and archetypical (infantile developmental interests) events. The applicability to artistic creations of this multilayered view of meaning, in the context of the humanistic, developmental perspective that characterizes the psychoanalytic view of mental development and functioning, is patent.

Although acknowledging the complementarity of developmental imperatives and the social matrix, the psychoanalytic emphasis is ahistorical and in that way asocial. In fact the social matrix is seen as dialectically determined by developmental imperatives in specific sociohistorical contexts. It is the understanding of universals related to human development that allows psychoanalysis to transcend epoch and culture.

Yet, the drama of the hysterical symptom exaggerates the relation of psychoanalytic meaning to psychopathology. It must be kept in mind that the structure of the psychoanalytic understanding of symptoms, character structure, and normative behavior is essentially identical, even though character structure and normative behavior are generally more broadly motivated and multidetermined than the overdetermined events underlying symptoms.

With regard to applying psychoanalysis to the study of creativity, the tendency to see psychoanalytic studies as studies of psychopathology is intensified by Freud's unfortunate term, *pa-thography*, which implies writing about illness. Yet the term *biography*, the writing about or the study of the history of an individual life, does not capture the unique contribution of psychoanalysis—that the subjective life is tangentially related to actualities. My term *metabiography*, with an implication of considerations "beyond" the historical actualities, is an attempt to include the subjective component in biography.

Another psychoanalytic legacy that comes from the study of the drama of hysterical symptoms is an overemphasis on the role of the personal. Early in psychoanalysis historical infantile events eclipsed the significance of the explication of the interplay of psychodynamic imperatives, the compromise formations. The emphasis on the importance of personal historical genesis often is seen as characteristic of psychoanalytic studies. Even though the psychoanalytic explication of personal historical genesis adds richly to the study of artists, the emphasis on genesis represents but one sector of the psychoanalytic study of art. In fact it is the study of psychodynamics depicted in portrayals, the psychoanalytic study of the art object, that have been among the strongest applications of psychoanalysis to creativity. The study of the art object leads us to an understanding of the capacity to appreciate art and the origins of creativity.

Psychoanalytic studies of art, like any analysis, are essentially reductionistic. The pejorative allegation of reductionism derives often from a misunderstanding of an intended "soleness" to psychoanalytic interpretation. Critics, in claiming that psychoanalysts regard psychoanalytic views as sole, confuse sole with fundamental.

Fundamental should not be confused with importance, however, because importance is a matter of context. Whereas identifying universals is of high importance when it comes to understanding subjective responsiveness, it is of less importance when one studies many of the essential interests of art history—the evolution of art, the history of the techniques of art, attribution, biographical studies of artists, the development of the history of individual works of art, the sociohistorical significance of art, and, to a less extent, aesthetics.

Iconology

Consideration of meaning is but a sector of psychoanalytic interests, but it is the sector that brings psychoanalysis closely in alignment with iconology, a sector of art history currently somewhat in disfavor. In his classical monograph on iconology, *Meaning in the Visual Arts* (1939), Erwin Panofsky, a founder of art history, provides a bridge between art history and psychoanalysis.

Panofsky usefully differentiates iconographic analysis from iconologic interpretation. Iconography Panofsky defines as the study of signs placed within art images to enhance and specify the narrative, a kind of semiology. Largely, iconography includes identifying such specifics as the classical symbols associated with mythical and religious figures, for example, St. Peter and his keys, Hercules and his lion skin, and the more or less agreed upon conventions characterizing various genres and periods of art. Panofsky's iconography easily accommodates the identification of the enduring, repeated, consciously and unconsciously employed personal symbols, the semiological signatures of an artist, that comprise a great deal of the psychoanalytic investigation of art.

Iconology, Panofsky defines, "[as] a method of interpretation which arises from synthesis rather than analysis" (p. 32). In noting the "equipment (required) for interpretation," Panofsky describes, "we need a mental faculty . . . which I cannot describe better than the rather discredited term 'synthetic intuition,' and which may be better developed in a talented layman than in an erudite scholar" (p. 38).

It is easy to agree with Panofsky that *synthetic intuition* is an unfortunate term in that it gives a vague, idiosyncratic cast to

what in fact is the stuff of psychoanalysis, the study of the subjective. Panofsky comes close to psychoanalysis when he describes
synthetic intuition as requiring a "familiarity with the *essential
tendencies of the human mind* conditioned by personal psychology" (p. 41). It is the "essential tendencies of the human mind"
that psychoanalysis attempts to make explicit. I hasten to add
that when it comes to the study of the subjective in art, psychoanalysis has all the problems that it has in clinical interpretation
and many more, as will be discussed later. Yet, when it comes to
the study of the subjective, of all the humanities psychoanalysis
provides the most encompassing approach.

In some ways it is unfortunate that Panofsky did not keep
the term *iconology* for the generic study of images and use as
subsets iconographic analysis and iconographic interpretation. If
such were his scheme, among the various kinds of iconographic
analyses would be the identification of personal iconographs, the
kind studied by psychoanalysis. Meta-iconographic interpretation of a work of art or a genre becomes a complement to the
wide range of interpretations that evolve through art historical
and related studies. In short, within Panofsky's iconology, I
would replace the term *intuitive studies* with *meta-iconographic
analysis* and *meta-iconographic interpretation.*[2]

As an example of the contribution of meta-iconographic
interpretation to iconology, in *Michelangelo's Sistine Ceiling: A
Psychoanalytic Study of Creativity* (1989), I elaborated on Panofsky's iconographic analysis of *Judith*, a painting by the seven-
teenth-century painter Francesco Maffei. In the Maffei painting
appears a handsome young woman with a sword in her left hand
and a charger on which rests the head of a beheaded man in her
right (Figure 1).

---

[2] Even though it is tempting to talk about psychoanalytic iconographic and psychoanalytic iconological studies, I prefer the terms *meta-iconographic analysis* and
meta-iconographic interpretation to denote that the system of thought is based on
Freud's metapsychology and the significant extensions of that metapsychology as
differentiated from other kinds of psychoanalysis, such as Jung's analytical psychology.

FIGURE 1.   *Judith*, Francesco Maffei (Seventeenth century). (Courtesy
of Pinacoteca Comunale-Faenza.)

Panofsky states that the picture had been published as a
portrayal of Salomé with the head of John the Baptist. In that
the Bible states that the head of John was brought to Salomé on
a charger, Panofsky asks, "What is the significance of the
sword?" In the Old Testament, Judith is connected with decapitation of Holofernes so Panofsky notes that the sword would be
correct for Judith. However, the biblical text specifically states
that the head of Holofernes was put into a sack.

Panofsky holds that the puzzle can be solved iconographi-
cally by "inquiring into the manner in which, under varying

historical conditions, objects, and events were expressed by forms . . . '' (p. 36). Are there, Panofsky asks, before Maffei any unquestionable portrayals of Judith with unjustified chargers or any unquestionable portrayals of Salomé with unjustified swords? From his broad knowledge of art history, he concludes, ''we cannot adduce a single Salomé with a sword. [Yet] we encounter in Germany and North Italy several sixteenth-century paintings depicting Judith with a charger'' (p. 37). In short, there is ''a 'type' of 'Judith with a Charger' but there is no 'type' of 'Salomé with a Sword' '' (p. 37). Panofsky concludes that iconographic analysis indicates that Maffei's picture represents Judith, not Salomé.

How might the psychoanalyst add to Panofsky's study? While not being able to help Panofsky decide whether Maffei was painting a Judith or a Salomé, the psychoanalyst, through his knowledge of ''the essential tendencies of the human mind,'' might suggest that Panofsky is struggling with combined, that is, condensed images.[3]

The psychoanalyst might suggest that the artist intentionally *and* unintentionally condensed in his painting a powerful Old Testament woman and a powerful New Testament woman. This condensation becomes evocative because the image contains *both* the evil capacities (Salomé) and the virtuous and salvational qualities (Judith) that reside in our ideas about women.

The dramatic emphasis on decapitation of men places the painting among a genre of depictions playing on a specific vulnerability of men and a specific threat poised by women—an iconographic representation of the significance of developmentally related castration fears. Closely related to such fears, a meta-iconographic understanding of the sword as phallacizing, itself a complicated defensive distortion, the feared castrating women, so easily presents itself that it might be regarded as trite. Yet, being trite makes it no less true or significant.

---

[3] Condensation, as a psychical process, will be discussed in the study of dream images.

Essentially the psychoanalyst complements Panofsky's study of the Maffei painting by identifying universal developmental and unconscious representations in the painting. Panofsky's iconographic analysis tells us about the painting and its relationship to the history of artistic depiction. The meta-iconographic interpretation tells us about humankind and art's particular evocative power.

These notions about the Maffei painting are offered as illustrations of how meta-iconographic interpretation can be used in consort with iconographic analysis to provide a fuller iconological study of a painting. The emphasis in this illustration is on identifying universal elements leading to a specific interpretation. No attempt is made to identify what is personal to Maffei in order to develop a personal meta-iconographic study from which a metabiography of Maffei as person and as painter could evolve. Such a study would require interrelating an extensive biographical study of Maffei with his oeuvre and his era.

Longitudinal and Cross-Sectional Psychoanalytic Considerations

The study of the importance of incidents in the creative person's life in motivating and forming creative work is exemplified by Freud's (1910) monograph on Leonardo da Vinci. The Leonardo study provides the prototype for the identification of the longitudinal dimension in the study of the artist.

The Leonardo study, both widely imitated and widely criticized, illustrates the complexity in the paradigm of early experience affecting artistic images (Gombrich, 1954, 1963; Schapiro, 1956). Most attention has been placed on Freud's suggestion of a relation between Leonardo's autobiographical account of a memory, most likely a fantasy, of his having been touched on the lips as an infant by the tail of a bird, and the characteristic enigmatic smile that appears in his painting. The markings of the smile are easily identified in the *St. John* (1515) (Figure 2), in St. Anne and the Virgin in *St. Anne and Two Others* (1509) (Figure 3), and is epitomized in the *Mona Lisa* (1503) (Figure 4). The interest in the fantasy is heightened by Freud's development of the possible relevance of the fantasy to Leonardo's homosexuality.

Another part of Freud's Leonardo study, one possibly of greater validity, tends to be underrecognized—the derivation of the pyramidal form Leonardo developed by positioning Mary on the lap of St. Anne in *St. Anne and Two Others* (Figure 3). The pyramidal position is even more evident in Leonardo's preliminary drawing (1500) (Figure 5) of the work now in the National Gallery in London.

FIGURE 2.   *St. John*, Leonardo da Vinci (1515). (Courtesy of the Cliché des musées nationaux [The Louvre], Paris.)

FIGURE 3. *St. Anne and Two Others*, Leonardo da Vinci (1509).
(Courtesy of the Cliché des musées nationaux [The Louvre], Paris.)

FIGURE 4.   *Mona Lisa*, Leonardo da Vinci (1503). (Courtesy of the
Cliché des musées nationaux [The Louvre], Paris.)

Noting that the representation of the two physically entwined women provides a schematic two-headed maternal form
behind the young Jesus and a lamb, Freud suggested that the
formal representation of the two entwined women reflected the
biographical event of Leonardo's having two mothers, the young
Caterina, who gave birth to him, and Dona Albiera, Leonardo's
father's wife, who raised him. The suggestion is that Leonardo's
concept of mother, the enduring inner image of the two entwined

FIGURE 5.   *Cartoon for Madonna with St. John and St. Anne*,
Leonardo da Vinci (1500). (Courtesy of the National Gallery, London.)

women, was made visible in this masterpiece. This meta-iconographic interpretation of the image is given further weight by
subsequent historical studies, paradoxically offered to refute
Freud's hypothesis. It now seems likely that the young mother,

Caterina, came to live with the da Vinci family to continue caring for the boy (Schapiro, 1956). Essentially Leonardo had two mothers much longer than Freud knew.

In a meta-iconographic analysis of Michelangelo's *pietàs* (1978, 1980), I used a derivative idea to explain the two Marys in Michelangelo's Florentine *pietà* (1555) (Figure 6). I offered that the two Marys represented the biographical event of Michelangelo's having had two mothers, the mother who bore him and the wet nurse, the daughter and wife of stonecutters, in Settignano who cared for him because of his mother's illness following his birth. It is of interest that in the Ashmolean Museum in Oxford there is a Michelangelo drawing (1501–1502) (Figure 7) closely patterned after the *St. Anne and Two Others* suggesting that Leonardo's painting held special interest for Michelangelo.

As a meta-iconological interpretation of the three Michelangelo *pietàs*, I suggested that the much discussed childlike *madonna* of the first *pietà*, the *pietà in St. Peter's* (1497–1500) (Figure 8) represented the image of his mother that Michelangelo carried within, a mother who died young and never aged. (It is equally plausible that the image is based on the young wet nurse, lost to him when he was weaned and returned to his chronically ill mother who was pregnant.)

I suggested that the *pietàs* represent the universal desire to return to the mother of our childhood, to begin again. I offered that the expression of this primal resurrection is depicted in the *pietà in St. Peter's*, is repeated in an intermediate form in the Florentine *pietà*, and reaches its apogee in Michelangelo's Rondanini *pietà* (1555–1564) (Figure 9).

The Leonardo monograph dominates the psychoanalytic studies of creativity giving an unfortunate overemphasis to Freud's hypotheses regarding early incidents in the lives of creative individuals and how they find expression in creative work. Nonetheless, elaborations using this paradigm have led to some of the most distinguished (and some of the thinnest) of the psychoanalytic contributions to the study of creativity.

FIGURE 6. *Florentine pietà*, Michelangelo (1555). (Source: Museum of the Duomo, Florence. Courtesy of Fratelli Alinori, S.A., Rome.)

FIGURE 7.   *Madonna with St. Anne*, Michelangelo (1501–1502).
(Courtesy of Ashmolean Museum, Oxford.)

Cross-Sectional Psychoanalytic Considerations

If the Leonardo monograph epitomizes the psychoanalytic study
of the artist and how life informs art, the longitudinal dimension,
Freud's (1914) essay on Michelangelo's *Moses* (1515) statue
(Figure 10) is the prototype of the cross-sectional dimension, the
study of the artwork and how it affects the viewer. Less related
to continuities within the artist and more related to the immedia-
cies of art's relation to humankind, the psychodynamic study of

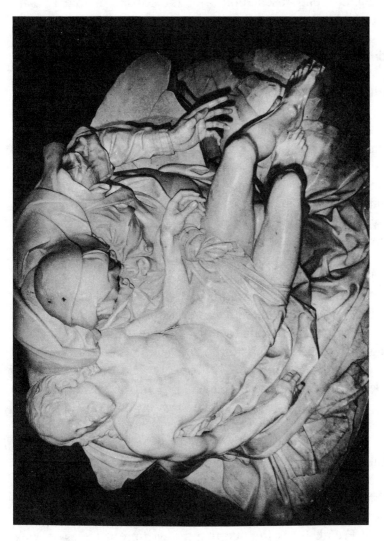

FIGURE 8. *St. Peter's pietà*, Michelangelo (1497–1500). (Courtesy of the Monumenti Musei e Gallerie Pontificie, The Vatican).

the art object offers opportunities to understand the unique place of art in human discourse.

In his 1914 essay, "The Moses of Michelangelo," Freud, following his long fascination with the Moses marble in San Pietro in Vincoli, concentrated on reconciling the apparent artistic inconsistencies that had led to a broad range of interpretations regarding the marble (Condivi, 1553; Grimm, 1900; Steinmann, 1906; Wölfflin, 1968).

Freud repeatedly visited the statue, sketching the positioning to study the formal relationship among the eyes, head, beard, hands, trunk, legs, and tablets. From his observations, Freud derived an interpretation. In Freud's interpretation, inconsistencies became reconciled as a depiction of a dynamic moment. Joining the interpretation of the major art historians, Freud agreed that the giant was depicted at the moment of his return from Mt. Sinai with the Decalogue to find the Israelites returned to pagan, hedonistic worship. Using details generally overlooked, Freud refined the interpretation and concluded that Michelangelo "added something new and more than human to the figure of Moses; so that the giant frame with its tremendous physical power becomes . . . a concrete expression of the highest mental achievement that is possible in a man, that of struggling successfully against an inward passion for the sake of a cause to which he has devoted himself" (p. 233).

Demonstrating the complementarity of the psychoanalytic paradigms, the Moses essay, although essentially a study of visual representation of psychodynamics, can itself be viewed meta-autobiographically (pathographically). Ernest Jones in a footnote added to the essay in the *Standard Edition* (Vol. 13, p. 234) noted that the essay was written at the time when Freud was "much occupied" with the fact that Alfred Adler and Carl Jung were forming dissident movements while proclaiming allegiance to Freud. Jones implied that the writing of the essay was part of Freud's attempt to deal with the rage a leader (Freud) felt and yet inhibited in order to protect an ideal (the psychoanalytic movement) when he was being betrayed (Adler/Jung).

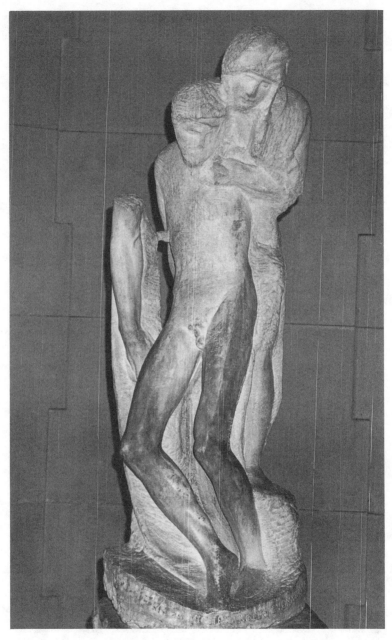

FIGURE 9.   *Rondanini pietà*, Michelangelo (1555–1564) (Milan).
(Courtesy of Mrs. Richard Frank.)

FIGURE 10.   *Moses*, Michelangelo (1515) (San Pietro in Vincoli, Rome). (Courtesy of Fratelli Alinari S.A.)

Jones' idea regarding the writing of the monograph highlights another frequent criticism of psychoanalytic studies. Although often alleged, hypotheses regarding motivation do not detract from the validity of what is produced. The validity of the Moses essay rests on its ideas, not on whether or not it was written in response to Freud's disillusionment with his followers.

Freud's essay is not purely meta-iconological for it makes a passing meta-biographical sweep. Freud considered that Julius II:

> [C]ould appreciate Michelangelo as a man of his own kind (violent and impatient) . . . (and) often made (Michelangelo) smart under his sudden anger and his utter lack of consideration for others. The artist felt the same violent force . . . in himself . . . , (but being) . . . more introspective . . . , (Michelangelo) may have (had) . . . premonitions of the failure to which they were both doomed. And so he carved his Moses . . . not without a reproach against the dead pontiff, . . . rising superior to his own nature [p. 234].

This sliding among multiple models derived from psychoanalytic theory loosely is what is meant by a psychoanalytic study of art. The meaning within the art is seen as a variety of derivatives of identifying evocation, universalities, personal references, and unique communicating symbol formations.

It is of more than historical interest that Freud published the essay anonymously as by ***' stating in a footnote that the study was not psychoanalytic, although "(the) mode of thought has in point of fact a certain resemblance to *the methodology of psycho-analysis*"(p. 211; emphasis added). His devaluation of the psychoanalytic importance of the essay reflected the early overemphasis in psychoanalytic investigation of personal origins and genesis. It was not until further development of psychoanalytic theory that the importance of the study of psychodynamics as well as psychogenetics was fully appreciated.

Method

Freud's footnote regarding method raises some interesting considerations regarding cross-sectional and longitudinal studies. In the largely cross-sectional Moses essay, the art piece is studied element by element with emphasis on details of depiction in order to develop an explanation that reconciles the most elements with the fewest possible assumptions, following the principle of parsimony. This method, like clinical psychoanalysis, requires repeated return to the material (repeated visits to the artwork) to correct the *observer's* tendencies toward personal elaboration on what has been seen. The repeated return to the artwork is of considerable methodological importance reminding us that in viewing art, a dialectic develops between what is in the artwork and what is in the viewer's mind, a point to which we will frequently return.

In the Moses essay Freud's use of experts is of interest; by and large experts provide the data.[4] In a sense Freud unearths little; essentially he alters the perspective on what is known as he attempts, guided by psychoanalytic theory, to reconcile apparent contradictions and inconsistencies.

In a longitudinal study of an artist, biographical and autobiographical sources become the skeleton and central organizing structure. Detailed meta-iconographic analysis of the works of art guide, underline, and lead to assumptions. As central themes converge between art and history, each enlarges and confirms the other. The reconstruction of life as experienced, the subjective life history, becomes the goal as biography becomes meta-biography.

---

[4] The use of references, particularly from art history, has caused psychoanalysis great difficulty. It is surprising how frequently the criticism of psychoanalytic studies of art centers on poor scholarship. When read carefully, the art historians discount psychoanalytic studies on the basis of errors in the art historical references, not the validity of the psychoanalytic paradigms used (Schapiro, 1956).

2

The Dream, Art, and Psychoanalysis

Freud in the *Interpretation of Dreams* (1900) took as a starting point that the dream has a largely visual vocabulary, the means of representation, which he saw as phylogenetic and ontogenetic. When translated to the formative arts, the means of representation is equivalent roughly to art modality. The dream as analogy to the created object is particularly applicable to the plastic art modalities, painting and sculpture. Although the dream is only somewhat applicable as an analogy to the large range of verbal modalities, poetry with its extensive use of visual images lies between the plastic and the verbal modalities. The kinesthetic modalities, music and dance, may be in a class alone and closest in form to creative thought.

As critical components to the formation of the dream, Freud described the day residue, secondary revision, and various ''dream mechanisms,'' particularly condensation. In her classic psychoanalytic study of poetic forms and the dream, Ellen Freeman Sharpe (1959) reminds us that in considering dream mechanisms the artist no more attempts to use artistic forms than the dreamer attempts to use dream mechanisms. These critical components amount to generalizations about dreams and represent commonalities found in dreaming and artistic creativity.

Condensation

Perhaps the most important mechanism in the formation of the dream image is condensation, an active, selecting psychical process that forms the idea as it becomes thought. Condensation is a refinement of the mind's inherent propensity to sort according to commonalities, a high order manifestation of the mind's inherent tendency to integrate psychical values (Breznitz, 1971). Condensations are formed coalescences of sorted image representations, an early form of thought. The dream image for Freud was visible condensed, multiple metaphoric meanings.

To understand condensation in dream image formation, Freud used as an analogy the then exciting experiments of Francis Galton. In studying physical characteristics and their relation to personality traits Galton superimposed photographic negatives of portraits of individuals selected according to personality traits. Prints made by superimposing negatives produced a new image. Freud likened the dream image to the Galton print. The dream image, like the Galton print, has dimensions, validity, and intrinsic meaning. Yet like the Galton print, it is but a surface reflecting composite layers. Using the depth metaphor, with the dream image each of the composite layers has its own interrelated validity, dimension, and meaning. The content of the dream is in effect images expressing synergistically competing motives, ideas, and feelings—multiple condensed representations of meanings.

Art, like the dream, consists of complex, condensed images in which the observer discovers coordinate meanings. Evocation in art is the observer's resonating with the meanings condensed within the art. Through both art and dream we discover the new and rediscover the familiar. Paradoxically, discovering what is within art and dreams is a discovering and rediscovering of oneself. At their fullest, art and dreams allow for recapitulations of the early moments of life as we discover ourselves and our world afresh, including, and this is most important, forming new symbols for organizing and expressing what we are experiencing. It is no wonder that through eons both the dream and art have been of inestimable value.

It is not going too far afield to emphasize the relations of economy of expression, a principle of parsimony, in art and its relation to condensation. Condensations are intensely economic, interrelated expressions free of extraneousnesses. It is the condensations of multiple meanings comprising the images that assure that an artwork endures and can be enriched by study and interpretation.

Yet a dream at times can largely be an overt and singular communication. This motive in dreaming was identified in an early paper by Sandor Ferenczi (1912), "To Whom Does One Relate One's Dreams?" In a parallel manner, an artistic piece can primarily be an overt and singular communication. Even though such pieces, like that kind of dream, may communicate more than what is intended, when the communicative function of the artistic piece is overt and singular, it easily becomes "hack" art or a propaganda piece of limited meaning, even when technically excellent.

Condensation and Ambiguity

Freud's view of the composition of the dream image raises as a central issue significant differentiations between *condensation* and *ambiguity*. Freud's theory of dream interpretation rests on condensation—the hypothesis that the images in the dream are visualized composites of multiple meanings and that interpretation is a process of revealing the multiple contents represented within the images. The art historical concept of *typology* is a subtype of condensation, often a personification of many related representations, for example, Adam and Jesus as *typus christi*.

Ambiguity when considered with condensation requires refined definition. Webster's first definition of ambiguity, "having two or more possible meanings" is close to condensation; yet, the topographic quality of levels of meaning essential to a psychoanalytic understanding is not captured. Although primarily derived from studies of literature, William Empson's (1947) discussion of ambiguity approaches the psychoanalytic concept of condensation. Empson delineates composites of meaning as giving a quality of ambiguity. Yet, like Webster's definition, Empson's concept does not carry the emphasis on repression, depth, and the dynamic interplay of psychical imperatives that control and select the availability of the various meanings that characterize the psychoanalytic concept of condensation.

The emphasis on dynamic interplay between conscious and unconscious determining meaning reached a psychoanalytic clarity in Freud's early attempt to understand the peculiar experiences of Norbert Hanold, a fictitious character in Wilhelm Jensen's nineteenth-century novel, *Gradiva.*[1] Freud (1907) wrote:

> There is a kind of forgetting which is distinguished by the difficulty with which the memory is awakened . . . as though some internal resistance is struggling against its revival. . . . What is repressed . . . retains a capacity for effective action, and, under the influence of some external event . . . may one day bring about psychical consequences . . . [a] return . . . of what has been repressed. . . . It is precisely what was chosen as the instrument of repression . . . that becomes the vehicle for the return: in and behind the repressing force, what is repressed proves itself victor in the end . . . when what has been repressed returns, it emerges from the repressing force itself . . . (and) even trivial similarities suffice for the repressed to emerge . . . [pp. 34–36].

> "Unconscious" is a purely descriptive term, one that is . . . , as we might say, static. "Repressed" is a dynamic expression, which takes account of the interplay of mental forces . . . [p. 48].

The contrast between ambiguity and condensation is heightened when ambiguity is used as Webster secondarily defines it,

---

[1] This was Freud's second and most extensive attempt psychoanalytically to study character depiction in literature, the first being his study of *Hamlet*. The novel was brought to Freud's attention by Jung because of the depiction of the interplay of dream, fantasy, and delusion and the role of the return of the repressed, not because of the novel's quality or importance as a piece of literature.

"of uncertain signification; not clear." Ambiguities are forms capable of eliciting multiple responses but contain no intrinsic meanings. For example, a cloud is ambiguous, it has no meaning within it. It is pure form in which one can construe images and through which aspects of oneself may be revealed.

The distinction between ambiguity and condensation is clearly illustrated when one considers the difference between the inkblot used in the Rorschach Projection Test for psychological testing and the dream image as construed by Freud. The Rorschach inkblots are chance happenings selected for being connotative. The responses to the inkblot, like those to cloud formations and smoke curls, potentially are limitlessly revealing of the responding individual. The responses are projections, constructs awakened by and assigned to the forms. There are no meanings within the inkblots. The response is essentially a monologue.[2]

The dream image and the art image are condensations not ambiguities. The evocative power of each stems from a complex process in which the viewer discovers the meanings "placed" within the image by its creator, a kind of dialogue through which the complexity of the meanings within the images are revealed. In this way these complex images are curious forms of communication, but with whom? The artist is not trying to communicate to anyone any more than a dream is a message. Art, like dreaming, is a kind of communication with an unseen audience, an

---

[2] This idea of monologue is not exactly correct. As we will develop in discussing dream interpretation and art appreciation, even the monologic self-reflections of response to ambiguity are elaborate "conversations" among various components within the personality, the introjects.

A somewhat related procedure for personality evaluation is the word association test, a method of study devised by Galton that interested Freud and became of central importance to Jung. In word association the subject is asked to suspend critical judgment, a limited form of free association, and in as uncensored a way as possible respond to selected single words. This form of exploration of the personality, rarely used today, is more structured than responding to inkblots, and the linkages among the responses are generally patent even though at times unexpected and shocking. Such responses to selected single words are different from discovering meaning in condensations, even though words can be condensations, that is, symbols containing multiple meanings. Generally, however, this is not what is meant in studying responses through word associations.

inner presence. The art and the dream are expressions of an inner dialogue. It goes without saying that what is contained within these condensed images far exceeds what the artist or dreamer "knows" or intends to represent in them. Each, the art image and the dream image, comes alive through dialogue. Viewed this way, a measure of what constitutes a masterpiece, as will be elaborated later, is the extent to which a given work of art is composed of composites of condensation, that is, free of extraneousnesses and ambiguities.

Yet ambiguities also may be used artistically and may characterize a work of art or a genre. Art relying heavily on ambiguity, although often fascinating and clever, rarely is a masterpiece in the sense of being ever revealing.

Secondary Revision

In a parallel manner, the dream and art have a narrative. The dream's narrative is the result of a complicated continuing integrative process by which the largely visual images of the dream are ordered within a linear time frame, and apparent inconsistencies are reconciled, a secondary revision. To a large extent secondary revision is a conversion of visual imagery into discursive thought, giving the dreamer the feeling that the dream tells a story. The story often reflects the central organization of the variety of meanings within the theme.

In art the observer also orders the images into a narrative of varying degrees of explicitness guided and directed by specific iconography. As in the dream, this narrative, often keyed by the artist's title for the work, provides an organization, sometimes a limitation, to the variety of meanings within. In art explicit and implicit iconography and form, just as in the dream symbols and form, are important linkages among the many levels. The narrative in both art and the dream is an end stage of various kinds of integrations at various levels. Although an end stage, the narrative in art and dream is not the final stage; it is the beginning.

The Day Residue

Highly related to the inspiration and at the same time paradoxically seemingly far from it are the conscious motivations for artistic production. Although apparently external, the commission of externally stirring events often are precipitating and organizing factors intrinsically interrelated to fundamental psychic imperatives within the artist.

A dream, like a work of art, often is anchored in current realities and social historical events. These events Freud called the *day residue* and they find their way into dreams often as the major thematic initiator. Freud demonstrated that embedded in the events of the day and the sociohistorical influences are the dreamer's specific recent and remote pressing concerns and ongoing conflicts. Heavily represented in these imperatives are early unresolved infantile and childhood concerns. Freud fully appreciated that as substructure the universal developmental experiences and tasks of humankind provide the general thematic organization of the dream as they do of life.

The central importance of the day residue is often rendered trivial in clinical psychoanalysis by the emphasis on exploring the intricacies of latent contents. In fact, the opposite is true. Freud's concept of *day residue* allows for a full view of the dynamic ongoing interplay of the present and the conscious and unconscious past. Such an interplay potentially allows a reworking and further integration of the past into the present. By anchoring the dream to the day residue, Freud emphasized the superordinate importance of actual and external events in psychological functioning as they reverberate with, organize, and are a dialectical part of the immediate and the distant past. The realization of the dialectic of past and present allows for new dimensions to enrich life's experiences.

In a parallel fashion, the artist in accomplishing his task consciously and unconsciously uses contemporary themes, conventions, styles, motifs, recognized iconographs, and the assignment, such as the commission, in interaction with pressing

personal imperatives. Joel Whitebook (1994) in his essay, "Sublimation: A Frontier Concept," also uses the day residue in dynamic interaction with the intrapsychic as his model for
creativity. He resurrects Freud's entrepreneur and capitalist analogy for understanding the formation of the dream:

> [T]he archaeological or genetic material, the intrapsychic life of the
> creator, which is analogous to the private dream wish, could be seen
> as the industrious entrepreneur who is constantly on the lookout for
> opportunities through which to realize his ideas. The public matrix of
> cultural objects, which is divided into different disciplinary domains,
> could be seen as the capitalist who provides those opportunities [p. 332].

With great wisdom, Whitebook cautions, "every domain at
a given stage of its development prescribes certain rules and
therefore possibilities as well as limits of the articulation to which
those private thoughts must be made to conform if they are to
become valid public expressions" (p. 333). He continues, "The
geniuses are precisely those individuals who quoting Castoriadis
(1984) transform the '*rules*' and '*norms*' of their discipline so
that 'other figures of the thinkable,' seeable, hearable and so on
come into relief" (p. 333). I would say that Castoriadis and
Whitebook are describing the creative in any field; although I
prefer to say *play with* rather than transform the *rules* and *norms*
and the configurations themselves.

In creative effort, this composite of competing and interacting motives finds integrated artful expression organized by
the universals affecting all humankind. Like dreaming, art is
evidence of the brain's extraordinary integrating capacity as it
consciously and unconsciously economically interweaves topical, personal, and universal motives. It is the brain being the
mind.

In a sense art is an externalized dream. Again this parallel
is more easily drawn between the dream and the visual arts,
especially the cinema, but in structure the parallels apply widely
to the arts and to creative endeavors outside the formal arts including science and business.

The Dream and Communication

Although Freud largely saw the dream as a visualization of the struggle between dynamically emerging unacceptable desires and wishes and consciousness, early in psychoanalysis there was increasing awareness of the communicating quality of the dream.[3] The question became communication to whom and of what.

Ferenczi (1912, 1913), a collaborator of Freud's, who made fundamental observations regarding the construction of reality, recognized the restorative value in sleep and dreaming. Without making a distinction between sleep and dreaming in that the prevailing view was that dreaming occurred throughout sleep, Ferenczi (1913) suggested:

> Some considerations . . . have convinced me that . . . every . . . sleep is nothing else than a periodically repeated regression to the stage of magical-hallucinatory omnipotence, and through the help of this to the absolute omnipotence. . . . Now it seems to me that sleep and dreams are functions of such arrangements . . . , remains of the hallucinatory omnipotence of the small child that survive into adult life [pp. 222–223].

In ways that Ferenczi never could have predicted, recent studies of the evolutionary development of dreaming have confirmed that the dream cycle is related to partial arousals during sleep in higher order animals (Fisher, 1965; Hawkins, 1966; Snyder, 1968). It seems that animals partially arouse themselves in order to check the safety of their environment as they sleep. In higher order mammals including humankind, infants partially arouse periodically to reaffirm the presence of the mother. This periodicity is closely aligned with the feeding cycle. Dreaming in humankind seems to be a high order refined version of that periodic reassuring reaffirmation of contact with the mother.

As will be detailed later, Donald Winnicott's (1953) explication of ontogenesis, the process by which self and nonself

---

[3] Unacceptable has to be evaluated in terms of the personality. Not all desires or wishes are acceptable. For some, even wishes and desires for pleasure are unacceptable.

(essentially the mother) separation and integration take place, is centered on the use of external inanimate things endowed with meaning, the transitional objects. The transitional object, an external symbol of the mother that allows separation from the mother, has been immortalized in the United States by Charles Schulz's Linus and his blanket. Winnicott hypothesized that for most individuals, as self and other become differentiated and integrated, transitional functioning and transitional objects become subsumed by interpersonal relatedness. Winnicott saw the continuing heirs of transitional objects and transitional functioning as the dream, dreaming, the cultural objects.

The relation between the dream and dreaming and the early reassuring presence of the mother was extensively studied by Bertram Lewin (1948, 1953). Central to understanding the structure of the dream was Lewin's (1948, 1953) hypothesis regarding a "dream screen." Although it is difficult to epitomize Lewin's rather abstract concept in a brief review, the basic idea is that the mother becomes an underlying continuing invisible representation in the dream. Using the cinema screen as an analogy, Lewin conceptualized the mother's body as represented by "the dream screen," an external but internal location upon which the dream is experienced. The dream becomes the day's joys and the disappointments brought nightly to the mother to have her enjoy the "good" and make right the "bad," to make the unjust just and the un-understandable understandable.[4]

This two-leveled structure of the dream is highly adaptable to understanding the created object and that which is made on or of it. This two-leveled concept goes a long way in helping establish with whom and what the dream is communicating with strong parallels to the created artwork.

---

[4] Using a similar construction arrived at independently from observations of children, Erik Erikson (1937, 1954, 1963, 1977) saw the "place" in which the child plays as representing the continuing presence of the mother to which the child brings joys to delight her and travails for her magically to make right.

The Conscious–Unconscious Dichotomy

A note of caution should be made regarding the commonly offered dichotomy between conscious and unconscious. As useful as this topographic model is for understanding a host of specific behaviors such as slips, specifics about the dream, acting out, character traits, and symptoms, as a dichotomy the conscious–unconscious model fails when applied to creativity. This caution about the conscious–unconscious dichotomy was strongly made by the art historian James Elkins (1994) in his essay, "The Failed and the Inadvertent: Art History and the Concept of the Unconscious." Elkins writes, "We can allow our artists to be complex, provocative, and genuinely intriguing, and at the same time use the possibilities that psychoanalysis has opened to us, if we refuse to be seduced by the aetiologies and personal narratives of clinical practice and if we decline to imagine a uniform, thematised conscious *or* unconscious" (p. 131).

The sense of fluidity of influence and the lack of the artist's ability to discern what is from without and what is from within is an important revelation in nearly every autobiographic description of the subjective experience of creativity (Kris, 1952; Arieti, 1976). The dichotomy is further complicated by post hoc rationalization and various "fillings in" characteristic of experience that is clearly unconsciously driven. The subjective feeling of "its coming from somewhere outside but inside" is frequently expressed. Often the subjective feeling is reified by calling it a gift, God given, or a visit from the Muse. The scientific lexicon too often translates God given into the equally mystical idea that creativity comes from heredity.

In creative activity the conscious and the unconscious are more of a dialectic than in usual discursive discourse. Thinking of a conscious–unconscious dialectic frees us from the psychoanalytic tendency to overemphasize the decoding of the unconscious representations and to equate such decoding with understanding the art object. Thinking of a conscious–unconscious dialectic also frees us from the pernicious tendency to think that creative people can explain their creativity or their art. One is reminded of the story of the abstract painter, who when asked to explain what his painting meant, said, "If I have to tell you, I must have painted it wrong."

Of course some artists have unusual ability to discuss creativity and art, their own and that of others. This ability to describe creativity and to critique art generally is independent of their creativity. In this role, artists are essentially teachers who use their experience to make their point. Yet artists generally regard themselves as rather inarticulate, particularly about creativity, seeing it largely as a mystical "gift." Some take their creativity for granted and think that it is an ability that anyone can develop. In general I have been struck with how artists feel that they are unable to describe or explain their creativity while often beautifully describing their creative experiences.

3

Dream Interpretation and Art Appreciation

A lthough it is tempting to contrast dream interpretation with art interpretation, the less precise term *art appreciation* is preferable. *Art appreciation* captures the fact that responses to art tend to remain on the more subjective, nonverbal level whereas dream interpretation is highly involved in verbalization.

The most important difference between dream interpretation and art appreciation is that dream interpretation is essentially dyadic, whereas art appreciation is monadic. Paradoxically, even though dream interpretation is experienced as between dreamer and interpreter (dyadic), dream interpretation is between the dreamer and himself (monadic). Even though art appreciation is experienced as between the viewer and himself (monadic), in fact art appreciation is between the art object, really the artist, and the art viewer (dyadic).[1]

In dyadic dream interpretation, the interpreter initially responds silently to the dreamer's images as ambiguities, forms in which the interpreter's personal ideas are construed. There is a free range to the interpreter's responses.[2]

---

[1] The interpretation of one's own dreams, an exceedingly complex process not considered here, is close to art appreciation and fraught with many of the same perils.

[2] A parallel can be drawn between this initial stage and the *wild analysis* of dreams. In wild analysis, the dream image brings forth from the interpreter uncoordinated, unintegrated, widely diverse, though not necessarily uninteresting interpreta-

In dream interpretation, the interpreter's initial projective responses to the images as guided by the dreamer's associations become sorted and coordinated. The dreamer and interpreter progressively and together discover the multilayered meanings within the condensations that comprise the dream images. Associations to the dream must be considered in the broadest context including apparently inconsequential asides regarding the dream; intentional and unintentional thoughts about the dream preceding, during, and subsequent to its report; body movements; and above all, the transferential context within the psychoanalytic process in which the dream is presented and considered. The process becomes a full working together, dreamer and interpreter synergistically contributing, guided by the dreamer's associations and the dreamer's and the interpreter's explication of them—a process facilitated by the interpreter's interpretation of the dreamer's resistance to seeing and feeling, a process easily altered and stunted by the interpreter's interventions.

In art appreciation, initially, the art images, like dream images, function as ambiguities on which an uncoordinated wide range of ideas, thoughts, and feelings are projected. In art interpretation, as in dream interpretation, this is but the initial responding.

Yet what are the corresponding directives, modulators, and correctives to the dreamer's associations in appreciating art? What converts "reacting" to art to "appreciating" art? To carry the analogy to dream interpretation further, what are the directives, modulators, and correctives that convert "wild art appreciation" to art appreciation?

Freud's "The Moses of Michelangelo" provides a prototype. In the essay, Freud describes a process in which he developed various perspectives by trying varying combinations to test ideas. He "played," in the true meaning of the word *play*, with

---

tions. Wild analysis is not revealing of the dreamer but of the interpreter. It is essentially monadic. It is the interpreter's projections stimulated by the dreamer's productions without the all-important directives and correctives provided by the dreamer's associations.

the image *repeatedly returning* to the piece as he attempted to achieve a concept that brought together seemingly disparate concepts. Freud was assembling the economic interrelatedness of the artwork's elements.

Art appreciation, like dream interpretation, is a gradual narrowing of perspective, a reductionism. Paradoxically, this narrowing of perspective is a "deepening" and "broadening" as less is considered (reduction of themes) in more complex ways (multiple expression through differing forms and contexts). In art appreciation, the essential modulating principle is the synergistic thematic and formal interrelatedness within the piece. The appreciation of the interrelatedness requires a repeated return to the piece. In dream interpretation, the modulating principle is the thematic and formal interrelatedness of concepts within the dreamer. In both, it is the interrelatedness of the constructs that provides the sense of conviction. As Richard Kuhns (1983) states, "in the encounter with art, control is gained through wide experience, knowledge, and the capacity to respond to the right things in the right way" (p. 93). More clearly stated and closer to my views is Esther Dotson's (1979) position, "Basic structural agreement between textural and pictorial schemes must be an important criterion for judging the validity of an interpretation. Specific details of the painting should also be accounted for within the logic of the whole, especially unconventional or unexpected details of organization and rendering" (p. 224).

Freud's paradigm carries a further implication. Freud's method was, without eliminating any expressive component, to combine each element of artistic expression in an attempt to achieve the most economic understanding. Each expressive element was studied to see how it synergistically worked with each other expressive element to develop and enhance a unitary theme. The essay vividly demonstrates the fact that in an artistic masterpiece there is no ambiguity, inconsistency, or extraneousness in the elements of expression. This view prefigures the art historian Staale Sinding-Larsen's (1969) evaluation of the works of great artists. Sinding-Larsen notes that if the interpreter has to "resort

to the explanation that the authors of the iconographical pro-
gramme or the artist himself were responsible for a slip [to substantiate a thesis]; such an expedient on the part of the art
historian usually means that his method is wrong'' (p. 144). This,
I believe, is correct but only for a masterpiece.

Although Dotson is developing a way to validate art interpretation, generally art appreciation is less formal, remaining as
emotion-laden partially thought out, yet valid, constructs that
only rarely are incrementally formalized into a verbalized interpretation.

It is the search for inner consistency among the constructs
within a developing interpretation of a dream or an art piece that
brings the viewer repeatedly back to the dream or piece. It is
remarkable how quickly and extensively our minds ''change'' a
given work of art.

It is well to remind ourselves that the dream, no matter how
real it seems or is remembered as being, is not a thing. The
dream is but mental images. The dream as well as the dreamer
changes in response to the dream interpreter's interest and responses. By contrast, art is actualized images. In art appreciation,
only the viewer changes. The sense of finding ''new things'' in
dream or artwork is illusory. The process largely is a dialectical
finding of new aspects of the viewer stimulated, coordinated, and
modulated by what is found within the dream or art piece. At
base art appreciation is dyadic. The viewer is ''reading'' the
multiple meanings packed into the images by the artist. Art appreciation is essentially a dialogue between viewer and artist.
Dream interpretation is essentially a monologue of the dreamer
and himself.

A frequent art historical criticism of Freud's Moses study
and of psychoanalytic studies of art in general stems from a
failure to appreciate that psychoanalytic interpretations are offered as complimentary interpretations. In the Moses essay,
Freud evolves a psychodynamic interpretation, psychodynamic
in the sense that he speculates that the statue depicts tension-
filled conflict among psychological imperatives. Implied is that

such psychoanalytic interpretations are integral with interpretations of biographical, social, historical, and artistic significance. Yet, psychoanalytically viewed, many cultural and social values are externalized reflections of primary developmental necessities, and psychoanalytic interpretations touch the infrastructure of biographical, social, cultural, and historical interpretations. In this way, psychoanalytic interpretations are more basic and appear all assuming.

It is of historical interest that Freud was reluctant to regard the Moses study as psychoanalytic. His reluctance reflected the fact that the study came early in his theorizing during the time when he was more interested in trauma, mastery by repetition, and genesis than in psychodynamics. It was later that Freud realized that psychoanalysis encompasses a broad elucidation of mental functioning. In essence, psychoanalysis is the elucidation of the interplay among wishes, needs, and their modulators, and the developmental vicissitudes of each.

In that art is closely related to universal experiences and primal concerns, the viewer is being brought into contact with aspects of himself that are fleeting, distant, disorganized, and often fear-laden. It is art's economic dialectic with the universals, birth, separation, dependency, autonomy, involution, death, fear, anxiety, and rage, to name several, that gives art its overarching evocative power and accounts for its enduring place in history. Universals must not be limited to themes, for symmetry, the elemental, organizing, formal principle of art may reflect universal experience. Increasing evidence suggests that the mother's face is the primary organizing external experience for the human being. The basic symmetry of the human face may provide the formal organizing principle to which all subsequent visual events are referenced. With increasing development, the basic representation of the self, the body, intensifies the importance of symmetry as a primal principle. In short, the formal matrix of all art may be the symmetry integral to the body image, and more basically, the mother's face.[3]

---

[3] These ideas are somewhat akin to Lewin's hypotheses regarding the position and underlying matrix of the dream (1948, 1953). Where Lewin suggests that the tactile

Abstract Art

The importance of symmetry in mental functioning parallels the role of form in art. This is most usefully exploited in abstract art in which artists obliterate connotative forms in favor of asymmetries and dysymmetries interplaying with symmetries. In the juxtaposition of asymmetries, dysymmetries, and symmetries enhancing the formal contrasts, color often plays a major role. Primary color juxtaposed with graduations of color interplaying with blacks and whites intensify the forms.

I suggest that it is the interplay of asymmetries and dysymmetries with symmetries that reactivates the early experience of ''reading'' the constantly moving, always communicating maternal facial contours that gives abstract art its emotional power. Paradoxically, the unconnotative *that* of abstraction becomes the *who* of development. The guiding beacon in all art is the stability underlying the instability—the mother's face reacting, expressing, but always returning to the expected, the symmetrical.

The Evocative Power of Art

The Masterpiece

Psychoanalysis makes unique contributions to the investigation of the evocative power of art. Patterned after Freud's (1914) essay, ''The Moses of Michelangelo,'' these studies explore what in art allows it to be and what makes it endure. Such studies approach a psychoanalytic study of what delineates the masterpiece.

---

experiencing of the breast during feeding is the primal universal external experience, I emphasize the visual experience of the primal (the mother's) face. I see the eye to eye, face to face visual contact between newborn and mother, generally intensified during feeding, as the basic organizing external experience and the beginning of the sense of external and other. Beyond that difference, my ideas are strongly influenced by Lewin's model of the dream as a composite, an externalized primal ''that,'' so to speak, overlaid with visual images portraying higher level conflict and mastery.

Psychoanalytically any artwork comprises a condensation of three interacting spheres, the topical, the personal, and the archetypal. The topical is closely associated with the narrative, frequently related to or dictated by the commission. Within the topical resides the ethos—the contemporary social and cultural influences as mediated through the artist and the patron. Julius II asked Michelangelo to decorate the Sistine Ceiling to proclaim Rome the new Jerusalem. Julius II's interest was political—to establish the secular and spiritual primacy of the Roman Papacy. Michelangelo elevated Julius' sociopolitical vision to another level. On the Sistine Ceiling, Michelangelo was to make visible the ahistorical essence of Genesis, the coming into being of humankind.

The personal in a work of art is the sum total of the conscious–unconscious experience of the artist. It is the artist's fingerprint, so to speak. The personal is a condensation of what the artist is, has been, and prefigures what the artist will be. It is for the artist at once immediate and timeless. The artist condenses the personal and the topical—an alchemy out of which emerges a new creation part topical, part personal, separate from either, and more than the sum of both.

The archetypal is the unthought, yet psychologically transmitted, timeless qualities that make the human animal a human being. The archetypal is the ageless composite of the developmental tasks and experiences that being human dictates. The archetypal is our ahistorical human inheritance, which gives form, direction, and transcultural and transoceanic meaning to all that we call human.

All masterpieces are great works of art but all great works of art are not masterpieces. A work of art may be great for many reasons. A work may introduce an art paradigm of important and lasting artistic significance. Praxiteles' *Olympia Apollo* or Marcel Duchamp's *A Nude Descending a Staircase* are examples. A work of art may be great because it depicts an idea as never before. Michelangelo's *pietà* in St. Peter's as a depiction of resurrection has never since been equaled. A work of art may be great because it epitomizes a great moment in history, the Eiffel Tower or the Taj in Agra. A work of art can be great because of technical innovation such as Caravaggio's use of light and dark in *The Calling of Matthew*, or because of the new use of a modality, such as Anselm Kieffer's use of slate. The development of a character such as Shakespeare's Falstaff is a great work of art. In short there are many historical, social, political, and artistic reasons why a work of art becomes great and attains enduring significance.

Yet even great art may be dominated by narrative to its detriment. *Richard III*, Leni Reifenstahl's *The Triumph of the Will*, the monumental David painting of *The Coronation of Napoleon*, and the acres of Ruben's apotheosis of Marie dei Medici in the Louvre never develop beyond their themes. Such topically dominated art, and there is no shortage of it, is essentially propaganda. Frequently great topical art is uncommonly beautiful, skillfully crafted, technically perfect, and thrilling to a fault. At core it remains hollow.

When the personal dominates, the work borders on the idiosyncratic and is of limited interest. Louise Nevelson's repeating patterns of composites of black wooden cells seem overly representative of her personality compartmentalization and early life experience. Work dominated by the personal often has a vogue and develops a following but rarely transcends culture or time (Oremland, 1985; Wilson, 1981).

Artwork overly freighted with the archetypal is legion, particularly religious art. Heavily influenced by myths, the told and untold continuing externalizations of the developmental vicissitudes of humankind, archetypal art often is patent, at times ineffably tender, at times ineffably frightening. Rarely elsewhere does art as explicitly enact the terror of birth, disease, involution, death, the physicality of sex, and the ecstasy of primal reunion as in Hindu sculpture and Spanish Catholic religious painting and sculpture. Although remarkably moving, at times strikingly repulsive, even though coming from vastly different traditions, the singularity of content makes for unitary interpretation.

A masterpiece is art of a different order. Psychoanalytically, in the masterpiece the images are pure condensations. The masterpiece is a synergistic balance of the topical, the personal, and the archetypal with parsimony and freedom from ambiguity and redundancy. The analogy to the dream begs to be drawn. Because of the limitless meanings condensed within the synergistic balance within the image, the masterpiece transcends culture and epoch. Within the interacting condensations of the masterpiece lie infinite meanings awaiting rediscovery. With each rediscovery there are new discoveries. In the masterpiece, time awakens newnesses and makes known previous unknowns.

In the Shakespeare canon, *The Tempest* is the outstanding illustration of the seamless synergism that characterizes the masterpiece, with *King Lear* a close second. In contemporary American drama, *A Streetcar Named Desire* stands high. In the plastic arts, as examples, are Michelangelo's Sistine Ceiling and Picasso's *Guernica*.[4]

Although the material for the book was gathered from work with talented and creative conductors, instrumentalists, actors, dancers, writers, businesspeople, and scientists as well as plastic artists, in general in my examples the abstract and kinesthetic arts are underrepresented. This underrepresentation reflects the kind of art and artists I have most studied.[5] Yet, and surprising to me, it was my work with businesspeople and scientists that primarily formed my thinking regarding what characterizes the artist.

Art's Provocative Potential

Art's provocative potential is unsizable. As an agent as well as an organizer of experience, art is potentially threatening with its

---

[4] I am fully aware of the limitations of my list of masterpieces. These few illustrations were chosen in that they are well known and clearly demonstrate the synergistic interaction among the topical, the personal, and the archetypal.

[5] In general psychoanalytic studies of art and artists, somewhat reflecting the theoretical unclarity in psychoanalysis regarding affects, are strongest in the arts that have narrative and in which the topical is orienting. Nonetheless, there are a number

content, its use of new symbols, and its proximity with universal concerns. Just as the artist must tolerate the anxiety of approaching the world anew, the viewer is also brought once again to the delight and the threat of the novel. Just as the artist must have confidence that what is produced is an extension that can be integrated into what is, viewers also must have confidence that they can "return," that they can integrate what they are experiencing to their own enhancement.

It is the fear of destruction of what has been established that explains those who are unmoved by art. To be unmoved by art is to be able to see things only in a specific, limited way, an essential rigidity suggesting early terror-ridden experiences with exploration. Parallels can be drawn to the individual with no interest in or actual disdain for dreams.

More remarkable are the well-documented accounts of attacks on and destruction of great works of art or of a genre of art. Such attacks remind us that art contains powerful threats to the organization of the self. Threatened with a sense of "no return," something akin to annihilation, a vulnerable self can feel it can survive only by obliteration of the disturbing agent. For such individuals, the work of art is akin to a nightmare ended only by fearful awakening. Like the dream, the art piece must be catastrophically ended, at times actually destroyed.

As an example of the power of great art to provoke intense, hostile reactions, recently in San Francisco a distinguished patron of the arts, John N. Rosekrans, Jr., was contacted by Richard Serra, the renowned minimalist metal sculptor, about a possible large-scale, metal sculpture for the Rosekrans collection. On seeing a maquette, Rosekrans recognized that the piece had broad scope and depth. As a major donor to the Legion of Honor, a nineteen twenties reproduction of the Napoleonic building, which houses the European collection of the Fine Arts Museums of San

---

of excellent psychoanalytic studies of music, composers, and instrumentalists (Noy, 1968, 1994; McDonald, 1970; Oremland, 1975; Pollock, 1975; Rose, 1980; Trietler, 1994; Reiser, 1994). Strikingly absent are psychoanalytic studies of dance and dancers, the kinesthetic expressions of narrative and emotion.

Francisco, Rosekrans, the grandson of the founder of the museum, considered that the piece might replace the inoperable fountain in the center of the large parking lot of the Legion.

The museum and its parking lot command one of the most beautiful sites in San Francisco overlooking the Pacific Ocean, the headlands of Marin County, the Golden Gate Bridge, and the San Francisco Bay. The parking lot is several elevations below the museum's portico and entrance arch that lead to the classical open court of the building. The parking lot, a vast asphalt area with a central ungainly fountain, is separated from the entrance of the building by about five-hundred yards of sweeping paths and stairs bordered by lawns and plantings. To the east, the parking lot is bordered by a balustrade and walk for viewing the panorama.

Rosekrans asked the director of the fine arts museums to review the model to see if the idea of the Legion site for the sculpture interested him. The director was impressed by the power of the piece seeing it as fitting well with the museum's overall plan to overcome its reputation as a stodgy and intimidating institution. The idea of a major, dynamic outdoor piece by an internationally recognized sculptor, born in San Francisco, was seen as a step toward offering art to those unaccustomed to or intimidated by museums. The chance to replace the undistinguished fountain with a great piece of art made the project too tempting to pass.

The sculpture, very much in a conceptual stage, was on a large scale. Approximately forty-five feet tall, the sculpture was to be composed of intersecting planes of two-inch Corten steel plates tenting upward in dynamic tension as an enclosure opening to the sky. The metal was to be left to assume its natural rust-red patina reflecting the materials and color of the monumental Golden Gate Bridge seen in the distance. The piece, mirroring the Legion, invited the viewer to enter its inner chamber for contemplative experience.

In the discussions of the piece, the sculpture was seen as an opportunity to link the classical building with contemporary

American life using Serra's renowned ability for abstracting classical architecture in twentieth-century media. Serra and his art seemed natural for the site. Encouraged by the success of the Louvre in blending contemporary with antique, the board of directors of the fine arts museums endorsed the project.

The Fine Arts Museums of San Francisco are administered by a complex combination of private and city funds and agencies. However, money was easily raised by private donations for the project. As a bonus, money was raised to include an excellent landscaping plan for the entire parking area. Being an outdoor piece, the sculpture was seen by the Board as a gift of art to all the people of San Francisco.

The first public announcement of the project came from a local art critic, Kenneth Baker, who wrote an excellent description of the piece and an artistic rationale for the site. Unfortunately the article was accompanied by a picture of an out-of-scale mockup model. A second art critic writing in support of the piece unfortunately intimated that those who might oppose the project were unsophisticated about art.

Immediately there was a major public cry of opposition. Such an outcry was unusual for San Francisco, a city that tends to be rather lackadaisical about art and its museums. The protest came from several quarters, strongly led by a local daily columnist of great influence who tends to sentimentalize in a highly winning manner about the uniqueness of San Francisco. Rarely was a day to go by that his column did not carry a snide comment about rusting junk, the artist, or John Rosekrans.

A loud voice of protest came from ''The Neighborhoods,'' actually a small group who live near the museum. ''The Neighborhoods'' are largely middle- and upper middle-class home owners who are politically organized and readily garner political power by identifying themselves as the ''grass roots'' of the city. ''The Neighborhoods'' carefully watch city government and support each other. They tend to be suspicious of City Hall and of the downtown business districts, seeing both as having the power. In fact, currently they are the most powerful political influences in the city.

The first line of protest proclaimed that the piece would "destroy the most beautiful view in the world." Playing on an antielitist attitude, the immediate battle cry, led by the columnist, was, "I am unsophisticated and I don't want that pile of rusting junk spoiling my view of the Bay." Arguments that the piece would be a part of the view blocking nothing went unheeded. The outcry about spoiling the view was interesting. In fact it would only minimally change the view, a view changed forever—and to its enhancement some fifty years ago—by the erection of the gigantic Golden Gate Bridge.

Many letters to the editor of the *San Francisco Chronicle* appeared, all but one in opposition. It is interesting that the sole supporting letter was from someone familiar with the sculptor's work. In the letters, several vilified the patron as a member of the rich elite who had no sensitivity for the simple few pleasures that were left for the poor. Many mentioned that it was out of scale and the equivalent of placing a large building in the middle of the view, spoiling the view of the Legion, even though the chief curator of the museum and the architect in charge of the remodeling assured that the dimensions were in scale and in fact enhanced the old building by being a counterpoint.

In other letters, the piece itself was vilified as junk, rusty metal, and monstrous. It was seen as threatening, giving a feeling of instability and eminent collapse. Often it was called oppressive. The fate of Serra's *Tilted Arc*, a controversial sculpture in New York that had been removed, was frequently cited without true knowledge of the nature of the controversy.

The artist was characterized as "destructive" and "menacing." "Put it anywhere but there" was a frequent plea. Some felt it belonged in front of the new San Francisco Museum of Modern Art, but "certainly not in front of a building with classical beauty." None realized that the piece was not to be placed just anywhere but was artistically conceived to enhance the specifics of the site. Several persisted in thinking that it was going to be in the classical court replacing Rodin's *The Thinker*, which was seen as classical, disregarding the history of the piece and of Rodin.

It was striking how threatening the piece had become even though it was in a conceptual stage. By and large the opposition was reacting to how they imagined it to be with no trust in the museum, the artist, or art.

Another line of protest was that the piece would soon be covered by graffiti and become an eyesore of the worst sort. Closely related to this was that the piece would become the local toilet for the homeless and others in the area. There was fear that it would become a homeless shelter. The reminder that art inside and outside the museum as well as the museum building itself must and would be protected was unheard. In fact, the piece as an important acquisition would command care. It was as though some people thought that once "dumped" there it would not be cared for as a work of art by the museum.

With regard to the piece itself, interesting was the fear of its size, material, and the sense of dynamic tension within the piece. The materials were seen as those of junk and decay rather than of the modern era. The sense of tension among the planes was seen as frightening, unstable, and menacing. Anal imagery appeared frequently in the letters characterizing the piece as a "pile of junk," "decaying mess," and a "violation" that was being "dumped on us" and that "despoiled beauty." Much of the reaction seemed a reaction to abstraction, newness, and evocative power. Without question, a banal reproduction of a classical fountain would have been welcome.

By and large the art community was regrettably and incomprehensibly silent during the struggle. Aside from the two excellent reviews by art critics and a careful explanatory article written by the chief curator of the museum, the directors of the other major museums, including the San Francisco Museum of Modern Arts and the departments of art history and architecture in the many universities in and surrounding San Francisco, were silent. Whether this represented fear of taking a stand and incurring political displeasure or lack of unanimity about what constitutes great art and where it should be placed, was unclear.

The Serra debacle, as the opposition called the proposal, was settled by Serra, who, sensitive to controversy about his pieces, withdrew his drawings. The museum decided that its "gift to the people" and attempt symbolically to extend the museum into the twenty-first century was not worth the political dissension that was sure to follow.

Despite numerous assurances, it was fascinating to recognize the intensity of the distrust (fear) of art, artists, and those empowered to make judgments about art and beauty. The tragedy of this experience is that out of fear of art and artists, the people of San Francisco have been deprived of a beautiful parking lot with a "bold and modern statement that would symbolize the dynamic art mission of the institution it faced and add to the cityscape of San Francisco an interaction with art that stretched the imagination" (Nash, 1994). The fear of art prevailed and future generations, while looking at a pleasant planting and a rejuvenated ordinary fountain, will never know what they missed.

Summary

Appreciating a piece of art, like interpreting a dream, involves sensing the multiple meanings condensed within the formal and thematic elements and developing economic constructs at many levels based on the interrelatedness of the elements. In some ways, art appreciation is the inverse of the creative process. Artistic creativity results in a new object; art appreciation is an adding to and a changing of the self. Art is agent of as well as organizer of experience.

For great works of art, the process is historical requiring interpreters and interpretation over epochs. Through being interpreted over time, a work of art continues to live and the full richness of what is within is revealed.

Paradoxically art appreciation is a kind of interpersonal process—a dialectical resonating between the personal and the transeonic within the artist and the observer (Oremland, 1984). Art appreciation is a kind of empathic responding to something from another. In fact, the word *empathy* entered the English language as a derivation from the German word *einfülung* (to feel into) to describe the ability to appreciate art.

Art and dreams, like interpersonal experiences, help the observer reaffirm old aspects and find new aspects of the self. Art and dreams, like interpersonal experiences, carry potential for self-validation, self-enhancement, and self-transcendence.

4

Talent and Creativity

In *Michelangelo's Sistine Ceiling: A Psychoanalytic Study of Creativity* (1989), I suggested that psychoanalysis makes important, perhaps pivotal contributions to four interrelated areas in the study of creativity: one, the psychoanalytic study of artistic form, style, and content as complement to the biography of the artist; two, the relationship of artists to their art and the objects they create; three, the developmental origins of creativity; and four, understanding depiction and evocation through the study of the art object. I propose that these contributions derive from three interrelated psychoanalytic paradigms: the first, derived from Freud's study of mastery and symptom formation; the second, from Freud's study of the structure and formation of the dream; and the third, from the psychoanalytic study of the onto-genesis of object relatedness. In preceding chapters, I suggested that the body of psychoanalytic writings on creativity is overly freighted with the first paradigm, that regarding mastery and compromise formation, giving psychoanalytic studies of creativity a strongly psychopathological flavor. A second limitation in the psychoanalytic studies of creativity is the general tendency to conflate talent and creativity.

Although often used interchangeably, the words *talent* and *creativity*, while reflecting commonalities, speak to differences. Talent is derived from Latin, *talentum*, a weight. The root word became associated with the capacity to make fine distinctions, to measure. Etymologically, talent is associated with special abilities, highly developed skills, and unusual capacities.

Creativity derives from the Indo-European root *kare* meaning to give birth, to grow, and to make. Reflecting its etymological origins, creativity carries the connotation of originating, the bringing forth of something new. Creativity, like birth, early on was associated with mystical interventions and divine capacity, the ability to cause to exist and to bring into being. The quality of something coming from the outside, uniting with the within, and reemerging as something new, is an intrinsic part of creativity.

Talent

The conflation of talent and creativity tends to intensify erroneous parallels between the psychoanalytic understanding of the origins and dynamics of neurotic symptoms and character traits and the psychoanalytic understanding of the origins and dynamics of creativity. The conflation has also encouraged quasiphysiological explanations for creativity to insinuate themselves early on in the psychoanalytic literature.

The most systematic presentation and the most widely regarded of these seemingly physiological underpinnings to creativity is Phyllis Greenacre's (1957) hypothesis of an "innate extraordinary sensori-motoric-conceptual endowment." The idea of heightened constitutional or hereditary general sensitivity or specific sensory modality, such as unusual visual or auditory sensitivity, as directing developing creativity, appealing as it is, when relevant at all is more related to talent than creativity. This is amply evidenced by the obvious role of constitutional and hereditary endowments as determining certain talents including sports, dance, propensities in acting, kinds of singing voices, and in technical aspects of many kinds of special abilities.

When talent is differentiated from creativity, among the most important defensive constellations motivating talent are various internalizing capacities, including introjection and identification. The strong linkage between talent and internalization, often intensified by the hereditary linkages of physical abilities and propensities, falsely promotes the hereditary view of talent. Even though remarkable family lineages of talent are readily traced giving strong evidence to the hereditary view, equal weight must be given to the role of internalizing capacities in hypertrophied interests and activities. When viewed internally, talented abilities, like mental illness, more often represent pseudohereditary intergenerational psychological perpetuation than hereditary determination. The role of other lower order defensive constellations, including various kinds of mastery, reaction formation, and turning to the opposite, are readily apparent in any study of special abilities, including performers, certain kinds of painting, designing, musical production, and writing.

Creativity

The conflation of the psychodynamics of talent and creativity is complicated by the fact that the psychodynamics of talent are those that determine the form, style, and narrative, that is, the contents in creativity. As previously mentioned, to a large measure, the confusion in psychoanalysis regarding the origins and psychodynamics of creativity stems from the fact that most psychoanalytic studies of creativity are of artistic contents rather than of the process of creating, an emphasis modified by Mary Gedo's (1980) view of art as biography, Heinz Kohut's (1960) understanding of the role of higher levels of integration of the narcissistic aspects of the personality in creativity, Gilbert Rose's (1980) psychoanalytic dissection of the aesthetic experience, John Gedo's (1983, 1989) view of creativity as an alternative to loving, and my ideas regarding art as a form of object relatedness (Oremland, 1989, 1990).

In the study of form, style, and narrative, the contents of creativity, the psychoanalytic concept of *mastery* properly dominates. Developed early in the investigation of the meaning of symptoms and dreams, Freud noted that much of the repetitive experiencing of specific thoughts, vivid memories, and dreams were attempts to neutralize overwhelming experience by shifting that which was experienced passively to something actively being dealt with. Freud saw the attempt to shift from passive to active as a fundamental principle in mental functioning, an inextricable component of a *compulsion to repeat*, a view he systematically advanced in *Beyond the Pleasure Principle* (1920). *Beyond* for Freud meant a principle of mental functioning more fundamental than seeking pleasure. In *Beyond the Pleasure Principle*, the repetition compulsion with its potential for mastery becomes a property of the mind, a prefiguration of the basic integrating tendency in mentalization, a psychological parallel to the basic physiological tendency toward homeostasis. When viewed in this way, repetition compulsion, mastery, and wish fulfillment become a continuum of the fundaments of psychical integration, and the repetition compulsion becomes the basic, common underpinning among character traits, symptom formation, dreaming, playing, and creating.

Yet important differences must be considered among these manifestations of integration. Symptoms and character traits are intrapsychic events and are intrapsychic continuances of varying duration. Unlike symptoms and character traits, playing and creating evolve external enactments, to use Kuhns' (1983) propitious term. Play—not to be confused with the stylized manifestations of expression, games—in its most complex sense is strikingly parallel to creativity (Erikson, 1937, 1977; Piaget, 1945).

To play means to allow various formations, combinations, articulations, disarticulations, spatial turnings, color experimentations, and the like, to move freely within limits, as Webster defines it. With its integral sense of freedom and trial and error, there is no word that captures the spirit of creativity as close as *play.* More specifically, playing and creativity are responses to and at the same time effects on the external. Such responding to and effecting of the external involves a synthesis by which an alloplastic event becomes an autoplastic enactment, a distinguishing feature of the psychoanalytic view of creativity (Erikson, 1937, 1954, 1977; Kris, 1952; Winnicott, 1953, 1967; Arieti, 1976).

Dreams, long associated with creativity in psychoanalysis and in literature, are somewhere in between internal events and external enactments. When studied psychoanalytically, playing, dreaming, and creativity are akin to transitional functioning and involve an internal–external mediating object akin to the transitional object (Lewin, 1948, 1953; Winnicott, 1953, 1967, 1971; Oremland, 1989, 1990). The internal–external object may be the critical component in sublimation, a process that Freud (1910) considered among "the most fascinating secrets of human nature" (p. 88), and about which there is considerable psychoanalytic lack of clarity (see chapter 5, pp. 93–95).[1]

Talent as a Defense against Creativity

A little recognized result of the conflation of talent and creativity is the recognition that talent may defend against creativity. Taking as a central organizing view that creativity is intimately related with originality, then the primary anxiety of creativity is the anxiety of aloneness (Oremland, 1989, 1990, 1994). Considering the anxiety of aloneness helps clarify why the latently creative may defensively bury their originality in the works of

---

[1] The term *object* in psychoanalysis is easily misunderstood. Originally object referred to that which satisfies a drive. With increased understanding of the development of personality, the term *object* came to refer more broadly to the nonself aspects of the world. As will be detailed later, there are important metapsychological reasons not to equate object with an interpersonal other. Developmentally, there is a tendency to minimize the role of the impersonal other, *the that*, in ontogeny. *The that* is specifically relevant to understanding the development of creativity.

another. Under the protective aegis of another, talented embellishments occur as long as safe return to the work of another is
available. Such improvisational moments risk little in that they
are fleeting, nonreproducible, and most importantly, apparently
a part of that of another. Using as a parallel the model of transitional functioning, it is as though the child out of the anxiety of
separation explores but renders the exploration safe by keeping
the exploration close to the mother.

Talent and Creativity

To illustrate the relation of talent and creativity, I present five
performers: a musician, an actress, a violinist, a ballet dancer,
and a comedian. With the musician and the actress, both highly
talented individuals, it became clear, as the psychodynamics of
their talent were explored, that they used their talent as a defense
against being creative. The violinist and the dancer, identified as
creative from early on, are presented to demonstrate inhibition
of creativity. With the young comedian, as the dynamic origins
of his talent were explored, sadly he realized that he was not
funny anymore.

Tom

Tom, a good-looking, engaging, slightly built, rapidly rising rock
star, came for consultation because of excessive use of marijuana.
Readily apparent under his engaging qualities were depression
and contempt.

In addition to playing with his group, Tom, a serious musician, was enrolled at a local university studying music. He had
a wide knowledge of the history of music and composition. His
main interest was jazz, which he called ''endless invention'' and
his chief dislike, rock, which he called ''endless repetition.'' He
lamented having to work in rock, but this being the mid-1960s,

there was an apparently never-ending demand for rock. With bitterness he gave a vivid, yet poignant picture of the world of the rock musician—set upon set, flashing lights, screaming girls, "everyone high on something; no one real; never sure when you're real."

Tom was an only child. His mother, a teacher, was away all day, and his father, a traveling salesman, was often gone. His childhood was characterized by loneliness and unhappiness. Adolescence was marked by an early adolescent fat period and delayed puberty. Adding to the misery of his adolescence, his father's drinking markedly increased to the point that the mother asked the father to leave the home. Tom began to have fantasies and dreams of his father being killed in horrible ways. One time, he awoke in the middle of the night, terrified and unable to breathe, horror-struck by the thought that he would have to live with his mother for the rest of his life.

He began playing his instrument, the trombone, when he was 7. The trombone had been left for him by a neighbor lady when she moved away. Although the instrument was selected largely because of its availability, he quickly showed talent for it and music. During the psychoanalysis, we were able to identify how as a child his playing angered his father, who complained bitterly about the noise and the cost of music lessons, and how much the playing delighted his mother. Embedded in this was a sense of power over his father and a feeling of alliance with the mother against the father.

In adolescence, his solace was his trombone and his playing took on a new quality. As he said, "I spoke to it and it spoke to me. When I couldn't stand it anymore, I would play. When I played, I cried into it." Gradually he found blues and mournful jazz and knew it was "my music." He found that his playing made others sad. He discovered he had a talent.

By age 18, he rejoiced over beginning signs of puberty and his body thinned. He played in dance bands and in some jazz combos. He became successful socially, although he never fully trusted any relationship. His shyness reflected social inhibitions but had its appeal. He was most comfortable when he provided music for others to dance while keeping himself alone.

In his psychoanalysis, he considered the intensity of his hostility toward his father and the subtlety of the early rejection by his mother. These themes wove into a clear view of a strong fantasy of having destroyed his father and having regrettably attained a distant, unresponsive mother whom he perpetually had to serve.

The role of the trombone as a symbolic penis urged on him by his mother and which he used to torment his father added a strong fetish quality to the instrument. This fantasy to an extent became actualized when his father was driven from the home and was to be reenacted in his group. At the time the emphasis in rock was on ''freak-out'' dress and hair styles. While Tom's group followed this fashion, Tom was clean-shaven with long neatly trimmed hair, and he wore Edwardian velvet suits. He and the members of the group recognized that he gave their group a specific appeal. In our sessions, we could see that he was enacting being the ''good boy,'' an asexual, almost feminine innocent actively involved in a highly sexually provocative ''dangerous game.''

As the historical determinants of the psychodynamics of the ''dangerous game'' were clarified, his playing changed. In his solo improvisations, he increasingly experienced a thrill and contempt as he heard the orgiastic cries of the girls in the audience. He was amused when he recognized the implication of the musician's jargon for a successful solo, ''getting it up.'' His highly charged playing won him prestige within the group, critical acclaim, and a large following.

The tone of the sessions changed markedly. Tom was openly contemptuous of me, especially of my work, which he saw as slow and uninteresting. I pointed out his cocky, competitive demeaning of me. He was frequently late for appointments, arriving sleepy and disheveled. He asked for changing appointment hours with the general feeling that I must accommodate him.

The numerous tours that promised to be exciting ventures quickly became dreary, timeless ordeals. There were constant delays, dingy hotels, all-night parties, and ever-present drugs. Our contact was highly erratic and it was difficult to determine the extent of his drug use.

His physical and mental deterioration were apparent. I interpreted his deterioration as a request that I intervene in his life and take over. Strongly, it was implied that he wished I would insist that he leave the group and music in general. It was clear Tom wanted me to stop his playing as he wished his father had been able to do. At another level, he wanted me to take care of him without his instrument, a wish that his mother might have cared for him for himself. At times, he realized he was testing me to see if I were the mother who abandoned him or the mother who cared for him.

During this tumultuous period, he reported a dream, which was rare in his psychoanalysis. In the dream, he opened his trombone case and looked at the instrument. He noticed that the bell was badly dented. He was so upset by the dream that when he awakened he had to check the instrument to make sure that it was undamaged. Throughout the day, he felt that something awful was about to happen.

He became increasingly morose and depressed and there was a second dream. "I was playing my trombone to a full house. I was playing pretty well. I noticed that my trombone was beginning to droop. I couldn't believe it. First the bell and then the whole thing. I blew harder and harder, trying to inflate it, but it became hopelessly limp in my hands."

The next months were extremely trying. Without question, he had lost his "lip," with little control over his instrument and dread before every performance. He incessantly blamed me for interfering with his playing. I pointed out that he was retreating from being the sexually provocative star to my dependent, castrated "good" boy. He reflected on his loneliness as a child and the long periods of practicing while waiting for his mother to return from work. Practicing truly was a tie to her, having her with him when he was alone.

Tom developed ideas that I was admiring his body. Alternately he felt young and small experiencing what he called "in-rections" in which his penis "shriveled before your gaze." Tom knew that the small–large oscillations referred to the trombone and was amused as he remembered that as a boy erections were often called "boners," further confirming a conviction that the trombone represented a penis. He ashamedly admitted that he desired me to masturbate him as an acceptance of his masculinity and at the same time taking it away. More profoundly, there was a strong implication that in the psychoanalysis he was attempting to create an ever-giving, fully accepting mother who would never leave.

During this time, deep in despair, Tom played very little. His disillusionment changed into stark depression, and he felt that he had lost all. He described a black void within. The hours were tense as he openly berated me for ruining his playing. At one point, he said, "I need someone so badly that I don't know what to do."

Tom talked increasingly about his earliest years. The main emphasis was on his father's absences. When Tom talked with his mother about his early life, he was surprised to learn that she had returned to teaching shortly after he was born. She attributed this to economic necessity, which Tom readily accepted because it supported his ideas of his father's incompetence.

As this was discussed in our sessions, he began to question its necessity. Hesitantly he pressed his mother for information and discovered that as an infant no older than 2 months, until he was about 3 years, he had been left with a neighbor woman, the neighbor who eventually left the trombone for him. At age 3 he was placed in nursery school. There were thoughts that the trombone symbolized a reunion with the woman with whom he had been left with, a "true" mother. As Tom pursued these thoughts, he remembered, when he was older, waiting alone for his mother to come home from work. He felt like a woman waiting for the man to return. During this time, the feeling as to who was father and who was mother, who was husband and who was wife, who was child and who was spouse became increasingly confused.

As these themes reached clarity, Tom realized that the fantasy of his father's infidelities and his intense interest in his fellow musicians' infidelities were related to "his mother's infidelity." He desperately wanted "her infidelity" to be vis-à-vis his father. Sadly he acknowledged that "her infidelity" was vis-à-vis him (going to other children). These ideas were greeted with rage, interest, and a feeling of increasing control over his promiscuous desires.

As Tom discussed these "infidelities," he sensed a relationship to his early "good boy" behavior. The "good boy who practiced" brought oedipal closeness to the mother and anticipated, sometimes actualized, fury from the father. He realized that there had been self-emasculation in order to remain close to her, and saw his late teens as a struggle to gain independence and regain his masculinity. Clearly, his fat period and delayed puberty had been unbearable, but somehow deserved punishments. He felt actually castrated as he watched other boys develop while he became grotesquely feminine.

During this bleak period in his psychoanalysis, tunes, which always ran through his head, assumed a larger importance. He advanced the idea that long before he began playing his instrument, tunes filled a void, "They're a private language with myself," he said. As the tunes were considered, he realized that a change was taking place. Previously the tunes had been those of others. Now he noticed that they were original. "They [original tunes] come into my head when I'm alone at night. They're there sometimes during the sessions. They occur to me at the oddest times. They just appear in my head." He began writing them down and orchestrating them for the rock group, and they were enthusiastically received. Using jazz and classical forms, he undertook major compositions. He "found" a classical trio going through his head, thinking it must represent a bringing together of his family. He laughed when he thought it should be a quartet to include me.

Tom's Talent. During his psychoanalysis, Tom came to realize that his talented playing had many psychodynamic sources that quickly and intensely became invested with conflicted aspects of his relationship with his father and mother. The trombone with its evocative expanding characteristic was presented to him in latency. He was to learn that its origin was more complex than he thought. Tom always had the definite feeling that the trombone joined him to and delighted his mother and became a "bone of contention" with his father.

Adolescence instead of bringing Tom proud manhood produced a grotesquely feminized body, a caricature of the deeply depreciated, castrated father. His despair over his having successfully destroyed his father and his fear of being left alone to ever care for his mother gave his playing a mournful quality that others could hear. He had a talent.

As his body thinned and he became socially sought after, playing allowed him to engage in, and yet to be protected from, relationships. Playing the music of others so that others could dance, while he felt alone and separate, became a profession and a way of life.

As the public's interest in jazz and blues waned, Tom was forced to play rock. The exhibitionism and competitive hostility thinly disguised by "innocence" could be enacted. At this point, his music expressed sexualized, competitive contempt rather than mournfulness. As had been the case during his childhood, he found he was the "innocent," titillating and controlling females. Girls fought for him and needed to possess him; yet all he could find in them was an empty servicing of himself.

In the analysis, as the incestuous exhibitionistic desires began to emerge, his playing became "charged." The punishment for the incestuous, competitive, exhibitionistic desires became epitomized in the "limp trombone" dream, after which his playing deteriorated and he was left feeling he had nothing and was alone.

Tom discovered that his cherished memory that he had his mother alone never happened. Instead, he found a mother who was functionally a father and a shadowy unknown "stranger" mother who had left. As the defensive functions of the trombone playing were revealed, his talent was severely interfered with. He sensed an inner void that was nearly personified. As he said, "I can almost reach out and touch it." He wished to return to his instrument and his playing, but they had lost meaning. Gradually he conceded that he longed for a "someone."

Psychodynamically, the trombone on a basic level functioned as a transitional object representing a union with the "stranger" mother and on another level as the phallus for the masculine mother. As Tom experienced the loss of the "stranger" mother in his psychoanalysis, the stark realization that his mother was not the mother he wished she had been, depression ensued. The experienced "black void" was the symbolic representation of the loss of the "stranger" mother, a loss never mourned. In a way parallel to the trombone, psychodynamically, the "black void" symbolized castration and at another level the lost "stranger" mother whom he longed to reach out to and "touch."

Tom's Creativity. Tom sensed that throughout his life, long before he began to play his instrument, tunes in his head "filled the void." The tunes in his head were transitional phenomena, residues and continuations of longings for the "stranger" mother. "Being lost" in the tunes was a reexperiencing of regressive union with the "stranger" mother. I propose that it was in relation to the composite internalized, partially integrated, representation of the early "stranger" mother that Tom's creations arose. The psychoanalysis, by reactivating and helping Tom work through (mourn) the early loss, changed the nature of his tie to the lost "stranger" mother and his relationship to these transitional phenomena.

Prior to the analysis, the tunes needed the quality of belonging to another in order to protect Tom from a sense of loss. As a result of analysis, a balance shifted from their being more of her and less of him to being more of him and less of her. They were original. Metapsychologically, the tunes became more transitional and less a part of the object; more the me and less the not-me.

I see Tom's expressions, "The tunes are in my head and they keep coming," "They occur to me," and "They appear in my head" as metaphoric descriptions of his sense of integration of the self-representation, yet with the quality of separateness in a space between inner and outer. This suggests that a critical component of the anxiety that inhibited Tom's creativity stemmed from basic levels of separation anxiety, essentially fears of being alone. This was intertwined with and masked by higher level anxieties related to castration, fear of loss of love, and various social concerns.

This view of Tom's creativity aids in distinguishing his talent from his creativity. Prior to the analysis his talented renditions were skillful elaborations of the tunes of others. In structure, they were compromise formations that hid and at the same time revealed, among other things, Tom's innovative contributions, which were encumbered by his need to use something from another. The creativity, though hidden in the talent, was at times given relatively undisguised expression in his jazz improvisations. He could allow himself these creative moments because improvisation by its nature is spontaneous, not reproducible, and quickly becomes hidden in and a part of the product of others, hence relatively safe. The shift toward being more original (creative) reflected Tom's shifting from holding on to another to a freer use of himself. This increased individuation manifested itself in many ways and was epitomized in his music when he discovered his own (original) tunes in himself. The elaboration of these tunes into compositions involved a progression that in many ways was a developmental recapitulation from early fusion–separation experiencing to highly differentiated cognitive discernments. The detailing of the progression of the development of the art object *as an ontogenetic recapitulation* from subjective inspiration through transitional enacting to defined object-related considerations is a little-plowed, potentially fertile field in the study of creativity to which I shall return later (see chapter 5, pp. 103–106; Rose, 1978, 1980; Gruber, 1989; Oremland, 1989, 1990).

Bette

A 24-year-old actress was referred by her psychotherapist in the East when she was offered an attractive acting position in a developing repertory theater company in San Francisco. She was an unusually lively young woman who easily made one laugh. She explained that she was an ingénue, renowned for her comedic roles. Through the laughter, it was easy to see long-standing, profound depression.

The depression concerned her inability to develop relationships that were *meaningful*. She laughed as she used the word, realizing how clichéd it sounded and that in fact the relationships were full of meaning. It was easy to see that she selectively found narcissistic, self-centered, egotistical young men who could not give, were not interested in commitment, and who were abusive. With a characteristic wry quality, she added, "I must be a super-masochist."

Her background was easily related to specifics of her acting. Her father was European-born; her mother, American. He was an antique dealer, dogmatic, authoritarian, and filled with pretenses, who openly delighted in taking advantage of gullible people.

The father and mother had violent fights in which he was physically abusive. The mother was visibly frightened of her husband's temper, readily yielding to his intimidation. In response, she would scream, sob, run to the bedroom, and slam the door locking it behind her. He would threaten to knock the door down.

She had a sister, two years younger. During the violent episodes, the girls huddled together, crying, fearful, and hating the father.

Reflecting her eventual career, the house, although filled with beautiful antiques, was essentially a showroom. The family was not allowed to use the furniture. In the dining room, beside the antique furniture, the family ate at a cardtable. The children literally walked around the edges of the carpets in the home.

In that the father would sell any item from the house without asking, the family never knew when something would disappear. At any time, Bette might come home to find her bed replaced by a cot or her clothes piled in the corner because the dresser had been sold. One could easily see the idea of living in a set.

In late latency she and her sister spent most of their time at the movies. The girls essentially lived on movie snacks and popcorn. As she grew older, she went to the movies after school, sometimes cutting school. She loved the happy endings.

When she was in junior high school, an English teacher took the class to see a performance of *Hamlet*, the first play she had ever seen. She was thrilled from beginning to end, especially with the curtain calls. It had special meaning to her that the stage, previously littered with dead bodies, was filled with the same people miraculously reincarnated and gracious with one another. At that moment she knew she wanted to be an actress.

She discussed her interest with her English teacher and was surprised to be encouraged. In fact, the English teacher commented that he noted that she had a talent for comedy and that she should join the high school drama club. On graduating from high school, she received a scholarship to a school of dramatic arts where she quickly distinguished herself. She was selected for a scholarship to an important theater group in England.

After several years of considerable acting success, confident in her ability and fully aware of the unsatisfactory nature of her relationships with men, a repertory company enticed her to come West as an ingénue. Once settled, she decided to continue her psychotherapy and called me. She worked well in psychotherapy and began an analysis. We could easily link certain aspects of her early experience to her acting interests and her relationships with men. Always she was the "sweet young thing" who could make people laugh at her and who never wanted or expected anything for herself. This was as true in life as it was on stage.

After some years of psychoanalysis, she was in a play in which she was the perky maid. In the play she was to exit in exaggerated anger, slamming the door loudly behind her. Over a period of time, the door became worn, occasionally opening on its own. A small hook and eye was put on the door to keep it closed. An older male stagehand was instructed to remove the hook from the eye just before she vehemently opened the door. One time during her exit, the door would not open and she nearly pulled the set over. The audience laughed. She was humiliated and stormed after the old man berating him royally for being "stupid" for forgetting to unlock the door.

The etiquette of the theater is that although a good deal of temperament is tolerated among the actors, temperament is never taken out on the stagehands. She felt terrible. In her sessions we saw that in the character itself, Bette was acting the way her mother acted (impotent rage) and that in bawling out the stage-hand was acting the way she wished her mother had acted with her father. She apologized to the stagehand who told her that he was sorry. It was all resolved with good humor, the happy ending she had always wished for in her family.

As we discussed the fuller significance of the incident, she unleashed an uncharacteristic storm of anger toward the mother. Although not excusing the father, she began to identify actual provocation of the father by the mother, seeing the mother less as the victim and more as the provoking participant in a sadomasochistic drama.

During this time she was rehearsing a one-act play about dissident students. The play concerned a malcontent, Sean, who developed a small cadre of radical student followers. There was amused concern that something must be wrong in that every university in the world except theirs was having demonstrations.

Sean took the affair seriously, becoming highly involved in planning a protest.

As Sean railed on about the injustices perpetrated by the university, his followers remained lackadaisical, going along with him as a lark. Sean seriously and intensely planned a sit-in at the provost's office. As it became clear that his followers had no intention of jeopardizing their academic status by following through with the plan, Sean became increasingly upset. In a climactic moment, Sean became furious as he sensed the waning interest of his followers. He stormed at the university and then at his followers. In the midst of the harangue, his former girl friend (my patient) entered. There was a moment of visual confrontation as she sized up the situation. In disgust she said, "You're just a blow hard." With that he physically attacked her. As the actors worked on the scene with the director, all confessed that they could find little in it that was interesting.

In one of our sessions, she told me, "We were going through it (the sequence) yet once again. This time it spoke to me in a *new* way. I knew exactly what it should be." She talked with the director and her fellow actors about "a new interpretation."

Why not develop it that Sean is on the verge of a paranoid break? He desperately and increasingly needs the students to agree with him to reassure himself that he is not crazy. In the beginning, the students are amused because he does not fully recognize the malignancy of his ideas. As they begin to sense that there is something wrong with him, the tension mounts. With failing justifications and increasingly wild attacks on the university and the students, Sean desperately attempts to keep them and himself from realizing his paranoia. His fury reaches a climax as the girl friend enters.

The girl friend is not aware of how far it all has gone. As Sean continues to rant, she in disgust says, "You're a blow hard." There is a moment of hesitation as he thinks that she knows that he is crazy. He threateningly approaches her as though getting rid of her will get rid of his psychosis. The intensity is nearly unbearable. As he is about to attack her physically, Sean suddenly runs out as though he could run from his psychosis. The followers watch in stunned silence realizing how dangerously close to catastrophe they all had come. The curtain slowly descends.

In the subsequent rehearsals, her ideas continued to develop and the excitement mounted. The actors began contributing ideas and the director encouraged her to talk with the head of the company to see if she could begin directing.

In our sessions, it was clear that the development in the play was a continuation of her realizing that she wished her mother had overtly recognized the father's pathology. She remembered many intense episodes when the father would wildly accuse her of being a "whore" or a "slut" because she came in late. Often the mother and her date would stand in silent terror while the father berated her. With this the fury at her mother mounted for being the "silent" accomplice in the destruction of her children.

In her acting, she found new qualities and broadened the range of roles she pursued. The rigid reenactment of being the one who submits, a characteristic of her life and artfully portrayed on the stage, became but one possibility as her acting range enlarged and she enlivened a greater range of characters than before. Even in the ingénue roles, there was a strong sense of seeing the role differently, a curious objectivity as she went "in and out of" the character as she developed the role.

In small ways she found new ideas in the scripts that made big differences in her characters. This creative ability rapidly expanded and was formalized when she became a director. As a director, she was excited to realize that she could "direct" actors through dialogue rather than through coy innuendo.

Although not as delineated and personified as in the rock musician, the development of an inner dialogue was an important characteristic of her creativity. As she said, "The words in the script *speak to* me and I play with them."

Discussion. The various compromise formations that determined Bette's talent, character structure, and way of relating to men were easily identified during her psychoanalysis. It was not until analytic work clarified that she identified with her mother to protect the mother from her hostility that her relationships changed and her talent widened. Freed from the bondage of masochistic reenactment, her acting became more creative.

In a specific role, which recapitulated her life, Bette saw new meaning in the material. She developed a new interpretation. As director, she "dared" to enter into "inner dialogue" with the playwright, first played out with me in her psychoanalysis. The "inner dialogue" with the playwright easily became an argument in which she had the last word (the happy ending from the movies of childhood). The actors in the play became externalizations of these "inner discussions" with the playwright. These externalizations (enactments) further evolved through dialogue with the actors and the play developed. As director, she became the parent with the actors who sees more in the child than the child is aware of *and* the parent who allows and induces exploration without interfering. The transitional child exploring (developing the interpretation) becomes the transitional mother to the actors and to the play.

Mr. Z

Mr. Z, an acclaimed virtuoso violinist, came to see me because of increasing fear of playing from memory. He explained, "Often I close my eyes and soar with the music. Sometimes I become terrified that I will lose my place and in panic quickly scan the score." Increasingly the idea of concerts with its requirement that the musician play from memory terrified him. He knew that his increasing "inhibition" was severely interfering with his career.

After several months of psychotherapy, he gradually recognized that he kept himself "glued to the score not because I get lost in the score but because I am afraid I will get lost in my interpretation." He feared that he would so embellish the text that the piece essentially became his composition. Gradually we could see that underlying this fear was a profound fear of destroying and replacing the composer. He laughed as he realized that he did not have to "protect Bach and Beethoven. The giants will survive despite my competitive attempts."

It was easy to see the psychodynamics and some of the origins in the specificity of his symptom. Mr. Z's father had formed a string quartet of which he was the first violinist-conductor. When Mr. Z was 12, he was good enough to become the second violinist in his father's quartet. Soon it was realized that Mr. Z's playing exceeded his father's, which led to severe personal and musical conflicts. At one point it was suggested by th quartet's manager that Mr. Z become the first violinist. The father became severely depressed. All silently agreed that Mr. Z should leave the quartet. His leaving was made easier by the fact that it was clear that Mr. Z was headed toward a career as a soloist.

As these psychodynamics were realized in the course of his psychotherapy, Mr. Z lost his fear of performing without music. Strikingly, he found himself achieving high degrees of embellishment and interpretation of the music that assured continuance of his stunning concert career. Of interest, when he played, Mr. Z always carried a "talisman," the gold pocket watch that his father had given him on his thirteenth birthday. The watch, a prized possession of Mr. Z's father, had been given to the father by his own father.

Discussion. Because of the circumstances of his psychotherapy, this is not a fully examined case. Yet Mr. Z demonstrates some of the characteristics of neurotic inhibition of creativity. Mr. Z came because of impingement on his creativity. What he saw as "inhibition" revealed itself as a specific phobia. He was afraid of interpreting the music. He saw his interpreting as improvisation and as an aggressive competitive assault on the composer. He feared (wished) that he could replace the composer. Even in the limited way that we worked, he could see the relationship of his fear to unresolved conflicts with his father.

In fantasy and to some extent in life he had replaced his father and he feared retaliation. At one point in actuality his ability almost destroyed the father (the father's depression). Even this limited psychotherapy considerably released him from the burdens of his oedipal conflict and guilt allowing his creativity to flourish and take new directions. As evidence of the place of the father in his conflicts about playing, Mr. Z needed to carry a part of his father with him when he performed. The watch, given to him on his reaching sexual maturity, to some degree served to reassure him that the father condoned his succeeding him.

James

James called me long distance in great distress. He explained that he was a principal dancer with a ballet company on tour and had become acutely fearful that he would drop the ballerina. I suggested he fly back for an appointment.

He is an unusually tall, perfectly proportioned handsome young man with a classic profile and a Romeo haircut. As he came into my office, before I could caution him about the half-step up over which many of my patients stumble, as though he were not wearing Timberline boots, with a slight skip he was over the step. Obviously he knows where his body is in space. I did not have to indicate the patient chair to him. He went right to it. Clearly he understands a set and blocking.

He explained that he recently had changed partners. He had been dancing with a ballerina who is unusually graceful and delicately proportioned. Because of his height and rapidly acknowledged extraordinary musicality and grace, he was promoted to dance with a prima ballerina, a woman who on point is 6'3"—an inch taller than he. Her dancing is reknown for the highly mannered, expressive posing of her unusually long, flexible legs, arms, torso, and neck.

As he grew more immersed in what he was saying, the full expressiveness of his body came into sway. While sitting in the chair, he began moving the ballerina's imaginary body, in and far, positioning her. This continued over twenty minutes while he talked half to himself and half to me. I was witness to his "playing" with her, outlining her contours in the air and molding his body complemental to hers.

Although what was being enacted is understandable in a number of different ways, it seemed that I was the transitional mother under whose protective aegis he was finding his way into and beside this new body.

I said, "It is a matter of volumes," borrowing a phrase from work with painters who talk about the volumes as they attempt to mold and complement figures and spaces. He said, "Exactly," and went on to describe how each time he must "find her waist" and "keep her on leg." He laughed and he said, "All that even though you can't see anything because of the tutu." Our work has continued as we explore other aspects of his talent, creativity, and the interpersonal impingements on them.

Pete

Pete, an unmarried, 25-year-old, part-time comedian, full-time waiter was referred by a psychoanalyst friend of his father's in the East. Pete was an avid follower of John Bradshaw, whose simple formulations about personality and motivations made him widely popular as a "psychologist" on television, as a lecturer, and in print. At the time, Pete was insisting that his father pay for him to go to the John Bradshaw Center for inpatient treatment.

Pete was a stocky, athletic, good-looking young man who was intensely anxious with a near manic quality. The initial visit was a constant diatribe about how I must be against Bradshaw because of the good he was doing and because he threatened my profession. Before the first visit was over, he stormed out of my office saying that he would never subject himself to the kind of humiliation that seeing me entailed. I had some confidence that he would return in that he left his backpack and sandals behind. Sheepishly he returned and I pointed out that at least part of him thought I could help. He made another appointment and continued to see me twice a week.

In the second appointment he told me that be belonged to Cocaine Anonymous, even though he did not use drugs, Sex Addicts Anonymous, even though he rarely had sex, Alcoholics Anonymous, even though he never drank, and Smoke-Enders even though he never smoked. He also belonged to several ashrams. In short he had many families all composed of the discarded and the downtrodden. Clearly he sought confession rather than conversation and association rather than relationship. Typically in each situation he became the bad boy successfully pulling for self-derision through clowning.

Pete was from a middle-class Eastern family. His mother, an amateur artist, was heavily dominated by his loud father, a salesman and a braggadocio. The father claimed to be extremely proud of his two sons. In fact he bragged about accomplishments and achievements that did not exist. Rather than building self-confidence his bragging made them feel uncertain about their abilities. "Crazy making," Pete called it using a Bradshaw expression, "I didn't know how good I was or wasn't. I didn't know up from down." It was easy to see that the father bragged about his sons to aggrandize himself. Although proclaiming how special they were, he essentially showed little regard for what they were. Rather than relate to them, he related to what he wished they were. Most of all, his concerns were for how others regarded him.

From early on, Pete was considered a problem. As a baby he was colicky. As a child, he was fearful, enuretic, hyperactive, and eventually "diagnosed" as having a learning disability.

The father prided himself on "never taking no for an answer." With the boys he was highly intrusive, never honoring any "I don't want to." He extensively used mockery, cajoling, and threats to force the boys to do what he wanted them to do. The father noticed that as a child, Pete made faces imitating him that Pete would deny. The father became infuriated, "Do that again and I'll kill you." Pete developed uncontrollable facial and body twitches that at one point led to his being diagnosed as having Tourette's disease and being given medication.

In our discussions, we could identify that the twitches were his attempt to control his uncontrollable facial contortions, which were imitations of his father's contorted angry face. His body twitches were condensations of his urge to and fear of striking the father.

In school, Pete quickly learned that he could make the whole class laugh by imitating the teacher's mannerisms behind the teacher's back. When the teacher turned around, Pete quickly assumed an angelic, innocent smile, which made the teacher furious and further delighted his classmates. A talent was developing.

When he was 8, he was seduced by Bill, the 16-year-old older brother of his best friend, Ed. Originally he described this as his having been taken "terrible advantage of" by Bill and that he was "scarred for life." With time the story changed. Indeed, Bill had seduced him by going down on him, but with great apprehension, he added, "the relationship with Bill was the most important relationship of my life—never before and never since have I felt as completely protected, accepted, and loved."

As Pete elaborated on the relationship, it was clear that the older boy was gentle, loving, caring, and taught him all kinds of things about life. Bill literally taught Pete to read, write, and play baseball, all in stark contrast to his distant, vulgar, competitive father and older brother. It was Bill who recognized that Pete could draw and encouraged him.

As Pete said, "I loved him. It continued until I was 14." With considerable agitation, after some months he revealed that the relationship was interrupted not the way he had originally told me—that he felt abused and used and when he was old enough beat Bill up. In fact the relationship ended abruptly when one time his friend Ed came into the room while Pete and Bill were in bed mutually fellating. Ed, then 15, was disgusted, "My brother and best friend, fags!" and slammed the door. Later that day Pete went to see Ed and lied, "He forced me." Ed said, "Do it to me or I will tell everyone." The coerced sexual activity with Ed continued for several months. Following the discovery, Bill avoided Pete. Eventually Ed stopped coming over to see Pete. Pete felt alone, frightened, and sick.

In high school Pete was identified as "a comic." Stand-up comics were gaining popularity and Pete was often the MC at assemblies and school events. As he told jokes, generally highly self-derisive, he would act out all the parts finding many voices in him. Often the skits were based on his family interchanges, scathing narratives in which he played all the parts. Over time, he developed a routine always beginning with a parody of his father's voice saying, "Now, Pete." He felt a power and an excitement when the whole room laughed at him and his family, particularly the father.

His father thought Pete had great talent and took him from agent to agent. It was acknowledged that Pete was talented. The agent suggested Pete tour the "volunteer nights" in the clubs. He gained some recognition, but was never asked to "stay on."

He barely graduated from high school with incompletes and gratuitous passings. He could hardly read due to a mixture of his intense anxiety and lifelong inability to learn. He had few friends, rarely dated, but was liked because of his sense of humor. Being humorous was a way of relating and maintaining distance.

After graduation, he attended some minor acting schools where his talent was appreciated but his lack of discipline and ability to stick to a task were major problems. His relations with his family deteriorated into yelling and nagging exchanges, and he decided that he would come to San Francisco to study acting.

He began working as a waiter and attending acting classes, but he quickly got into competitive struggles with his male teachers and older male classmates. He went from waiter job to waiter job with minimal success in his volunteer night stand-up comic gigs.

He sank lower and lower into despair, living with various difficult roommates and finding solace only in his "groups" and watching Bradshaw on television. "Crazy making," "dysfunctional family," and "inner child" became mantras and inspired hope. Near suicide, he pleaded with his father to send him to the Bradshaw inpatient center and the father sought the advice of a psychoanalyst friend. The father contacted me to ask if I could help. The father seemed more concerned about saving the cost of the Bradshaw Center than helping his son.

With me, Pete was always the mimic and I frequently shifted from being amused to being annoyed by his almost constant imitations of me, always mimicking my most unattractive mannerisms. He could "get off" on almost any word, quickly and cleverly playing with the word to make fun of what I was saying.

Largely we talked about his consciously and unconsciously acting out the parts of the members of his family as he retold family interactions finding their voices within himself. The intensity of his anger toward his father at times defied words. Largely he hated the father for "what he did to me." Any mention of the mother met with, "She is nothing. She only thinks what he lets her think." He saw her and himself as but "containers of what he put in us."

One time the father called saying that he wanted to visit Pete in San Francisco. Essentially he told Pete that he was coming. Pete discussed the call and the idea with me. It was clear that Pete was not ready for a visit. He told his father that I did not think he was ready for a visit. The father yelled, "I pay him and he says I can't visit," slamming down the telephone. Shortly thereafter the father called me. He was overly courteous. As I went over the details, he kept coming back to, "Well I am not sure I can take your advice," thereby reopening the discussion. Perhaps ten times, he came back to, "Why can't he see his father?" I had a vivid sense of how intrusive the father's persistence was and how impotent one felt with him. No matter what was said, it was going to be his way. The father did not visit and increased his complaints about the cost of the psychotherapy insisting that the sessions be reduced to once a week.

The interchange between the father and me was much discussed. Pete took delight in telling me all the vile names that his
father called me. We discussed his vulnerability and helplessness
before the father's perseverance and his delight in imagining that
I too had become a helpless victim of it. We also talked about
the peculiar identification that he made with his father to protect
himself from the onslaught. Always he knew that he could "act
like" the father, but now it frightened him to realize that in core
ways he was like the father. He, like the father, could see things
only one way—his way. He saw that there was a strong relation
to that trait and his getting into altercations with his bosses and
being unable to hold a job. He also realized that his learning
difficulties came from the fact that he, like the father, could not
be told anything.

The sessions changed to discussion of his finding himself
acting like his father even when he did not want to. He began
to see that "acting like" the father gave him some control over
his sense of being like the father. He had read about identification
with the aggressor and knew that it applied to him with an increasing sense that he shifted "passive to active."

With time, Pete became less anxious and was steadily employed as a waiter. He lost his zest for being a comic and realized
that he would never be an actor. "I'm just not funny anymore,"
he lamented. He gained weight and was socially isolated, usually
talking to friends only on the telephone. He slowly realized that
he was all but uneducated. There is some hope that he may go
to school to become a graphic artist developing the old talent
recognized and nurtured by Bill.

Discussion. Pete unfortunately represents a talent that was heavily dependent on identification with the aggressor, turning passive to active and near manic anxiety. Although played out with
limitless variations, he had but one skit and that was the persis-
tent, self-centered father coping with the exasperated and exas-
perating son. The skit was hilarious when he was actively living
it and playing it before peers who in various ways were living
it. However, the theme and form were fixed.

Analysis, rather than freeing his comedic quality and allowing it to broaden and develop as it did for Bette, the actress, brought the limited nature of the talent to light revealing its singular meaning. As he saw the extent to which his father was unable to relate to him, he fought less in his mind for contact with the father. Steadily the father diminished in importance in his functioning and the skit became hackneyed and anachronistic. His neurotically limited education caught up with him and he found that doors were closed. He discovered that he had but one trade, being a waiter. At times he pretended that he was an actor waiting on tables but more and more realized that he was a waiter.

In his ability to draw, there is a small ray of hope, interestingly stemming from the preadolescent homosexual relationship with Bill and possibly an identification with the mother. Whether he will ever risk going to school to learn graphic arts somewhat depends on the abilities of his psychotherapist.

Summary

In an attempt to explore the relation of talent and creativity, I have described psychoanalytic work with five performers. The rock musician, the actress, and the comic presented essentially with interpersonal problems. The violinist and the dancer presented with a specific symptom regarding creativity.

The psychodynamics of the talent of the rock musician, the actress, and the comedian were patent in terms of their conflicts, reaction formations, compromise formations, ego inhibitions, and organized and elaborated reenactments. It is unclear how these psychodynamic compromises became talents rather than neurotic symptoms even though each patient had concurrent and related characterological symptomatology.

Striking in each case was the role of a someone who acknowledged and in a way directed the development of their special abilities. The importance of another in the development of talent underlines the role that incorporation, particularly identification, plays in talent, and is similar to but psychodynamically different from the role of the ''patron,'' as I view it, in creativity (Oremland, 1989, 1990).

In talent the other provides form and content to the unusual ability. In creativity, the other is a recreation of the transitional mother, a protective aegis under which exploration (separation) with safe reunion can occur as vividly enacted by the dancer. Although we were unable to study it fully, it is most likely with the violinist that the father was the transitional mother (the patron), whose subtle transitional functioning was interfered with by reemergence of oedipal conflicts.

Of special interest in the exploration of talent and creativity was that the creativity of the rock musician and the actress was hidden (defended against) in the talent, given only brief and disguised expression, providing an exceptional quality to their work. In the violinist, the creativity from early on was strikingly apparent only subsequently ''inhibited'' by neurotic conflicts. From the beginning, the comic's work, although delightful, was repetitious and narrow. His talent was almost exclusively motivated by his highly conflicted relationship with the father. The talent essentially rested on low-level defenses—changing passive to active, reaction formation, and incorporation.

The creativity in the rock musician and actress was freed by specific psychoanalytic work largely centered on resolving the ambivalence toward the mother with lessened fears of being alone. In the violinist the neurotic fears markedly diminished as he understood the relationship of his fears and the attendant inhibition to his desire to replace and his fear of retaliation from the vanquished father. The dancer, it seems, needed only a protective aegis, a transitional mother, with whom he could safely explore the volumetric complement of his body and that of his new partner.

In the two performers who ''hid'' their creativity, when freed their creativity was characterized by attaining a kind of inner dialogue, a quality the violinist had possessed from early on that was threatened by his neurosis. In the comic, the routines, although varying, in response to the audience, and at times led by the audience, largely reflected repetitive exaggerations of experience and a remarkable but limited facility to reexternalize.

Developmentally the inner dialogue of creativity is a continuation of transitional functioning, a form of object relatedness. Psychodynamically talent rests on a variety of varying levels of defensive compromises (Winnicott, 1953; Rose, 1978; Oremland, 1989, 1990). In this distinction may lie useful differentiations between sublimation and its affinity to creativity and defensive capacity and its place in talent, as will be developed later (see chapter 5, pp. 93–95).

The psychoanalytic experience with these individuals adds increasing conviction to our confidence that creativity is not imperiled by psychoanalysis. In fact, like any aspect of object relatedness, creativity is enhanced by psychoanalysis.

Yet the situation with regard to talent and psychoanalysis is not as sanguine. With talent, the effect of psychoanalysis depends on the specifics of the defensive dynamics involved. Most likely, the more the talent is given form and content by identifications and other higher level defenses, the less likely the talent will be negatively influenced by psychoanalysis. Yet, as with Pete, the more the talent rests on lower level defensive functioning, reaction formation, and the like, the greater is the potential for psychoanalysis to affect the talent adversely.

5

Creativity and Relatedness

Although the word *artist* tends to conjure up painters and sculptors, by now it must be clear that I use the word in a broad but special sense. Like Greenacre (1957), I have in mind creative individuals regardless of field or medium who by virtue of their originality and broadly encompassing, exceptional qualities and capacities are distinguished from, and largely recognized as being distinguished from, their cohorts. The creative individuals, be they painters, writers, teachers, scientists, or businesspeople, are the artists in their fields.

Creativity and *Object* Relatedness

In the interest of making the psychoanalytic metapsychology parallel the natural sciences, reflecting the early twentieth century, Freud defined *object* within a mechanistic lexicon.[1] Originally derived from psychoanalytic drive theory, *object* referred to an agent, generally an external agent, of satisfaction through reduction of drive tension. As a basic model, drive theory employed

---

[1] In that there are many connotations to the use of the word *object*, including the use of the term for a nonspecified, often pejoratively considered depersonalized thing, in this discussion, I italicize the term to indicate *object* as a specific psychoanalytic metapsychological construct. In writing about art, there is also the confusing coincidence that the term is used for the product of art, the art object.

hunger (drive) in the infant and its satiation by the breast (*object*). Hunger was seen as a physiological event "driving" the organism toward an external agent that potentially could reduce, in Freud's term, the *unpleasure* of drive tension. The agent of reduction of the drive was the *object* of the drive.

In this early model, it was hypothesized that the offered breast was initially experienced as "appearing" because of need and only progressively became experienced as coming from without. As prototype, Freud suggested that in response to hunger, with development the *idea* of breast as *object* comes into being. The *idea* of breast is produced by the drive and at the same time allows for a delay in satisfaction. In short, the formation of thought is related to the tension between drive and satisfaction. With development and maturation the physiological event becomes a complex psychophysiological process. Quickly the psychophysiological process becomes a sociopsychophysiological complex.

With increased sophistication in psychoanalytic theorizing and with increased knowledge of development and maturation, the view of what constituted drive expanded and the importance and complexity of the concept *object* increased. Psychodynamically, with development and maturation the external satisfiers become specific, stable, and more generalized internalized *object* representations, intrapsychic entities with increasing multiple ideational components. For most individuals, the internalized *object* representations related to responsiveness, stability, and continuity (somewhat under the aegis of satiation and deprivation) through a complex process of projections, internalizations, reprojections, and reinternalizations are organized around the internalized experience of the activities and person of the mother. With development and maturation, the internalized *object* representations become relatively enduring constellations of concepts of persons that have become endowed with meaning. Such meaning ranges from those associated with basic physiological need fulfillments to high-level, ethereal wishes associated with self-definition and self-validation.

Freud fortunately maintained the generic concept of *object* in these developmental systems rather than using the more limited concept of interpersonal other. By not limiting *object* to interpersonal other, Freud allows the concept of *object* to accommodate the gathering descriptions of the complex developmental processes by which the self and other emerge as integrated differentiated concepts from an undifferentiated primal psychical matrix.[2] It is in the progressive definition, differentiation, and integration of self and *object* that connotative *things* endowed with meaning play an important part. Such connotative things, the *that*, are the developmental forerunners of the culturally important things including the art object.

This abstract discourse on the concept *object* in psychoanalysis is necessary to understand the relation of creativity to ontogeny. My thesis is that for most individuals *object* becomes relatively synonymous with person and *object* relatedness relatively synonymous with interpersonal relatedness; however, in creative people, the agents, processes, and resultants are different. For creative individuals, *object* and person and *object* relatedness and interpersonal relatedness are not as synonymous as they are for the less gifted. In essence, creative individuals relate to a greater array and different order of *objects* beyond the interpersonal *objects* for self-expression, self-validation, self-verification, and self-transcendence.

Emphasizing the role of the dialectical creation of self and *object* in studying creativity marks an important departure from and an important addition to Freud's early emphasis on the role of mastery and defense in creativity. Emphasizing the development of self and *object* in understanding creativity broadens our

---

[2] Recent infant observation research has called the idea of the primal psychical matrix into question (Kagan, Kearsley, and Zelazo, 1978; Kagan, 1984; Stern, 1985). These researchers demonstrated that earlier than previously thought, infants are able to make important differentiations of forms, textures, shapes, sounds, and colors. Yet, the idea of the primal matrix seems close to the way early experiences are held in memory, reflecting retrospective elaboration, distortion, and alterations. The idea of the primal matrix remains close to the way we feel early life was experienced even though it may not be the way it was experienced.

perspective and allows us to go beyond the psychoanalytic study of themes, contents, and forms and their relation to events in the artist's life. The study of creativity in relation to ontogenesis allows us: (1) to appreciate the source of the originality of creativity; (2) to encompass a broader psychoanalytic consideration of the development of creativity; (3) to sense more broadly the importance of art as *object* to the artist; (4) to understand the fact that creativity occurs early and generally continues throughout a lifetime; (5) to identify the intrapsychic "location" of creativity; (6) to elucidate the "audience" in creativity—the *that* out there and yet inside, that is being communicated within creativity; (7) to understand the role of the patron; (8) to enlarge our view of the nature of the art object; and (9) to provide a more precise developmental understanding of sublimation.

The Relation of the Artist to Art

The psychoanalytic study of the relation of the artist to art began with Greenacre's (1957) paper, "The Childhood of the Artist." Following in the tradition of James Joyce, Greenacre attempts a description of the childhood of the artist. Her description allows for speculation about, among other things, qualitative differences in the *object* relationships of the creative person as compared with the less gifted. Greenacre hypothesizes for the artist an "innate extraordinary sensori-motoric-conceptual endowment" that results in a reality that "is different from that of the less gifted person. . . . In the markedly creative person experiences are multidimensional, with the resonance of imagery. . . . " Of great importance, she states, "Even personal relationships are . . . invested with interest in many alternative figures and forms" (p. 131). In short, the interpersonal world of the artist is but a part of a larger world of configurations, colors, tones, forms, and the like and not as singular and central as it is for most individuals.

Greenacre essentially describes for the artist a different order of *object* relatedness that she calls *collective alternates*. The best view of what she had in mind is revealed in her vivid and often quoted metaphor, "The artist has a love affair with the world." Although I find Greenacre's quasi-neurological underpinning, her "innate extraordinary sensori-motoric-conceptual endowment," limited and limiting, I agree that the artist relates to a world comprised of a greater panoply of *objects* than the usual interpersonal *objects* for gratification, expression, self-validation, self-verification, and self-transcendence.

It is because of the creative individual's involvement with this broader range of *objects*, the *collective alternates*, as the main *objects* through which the artist defines, verifies, and replenishes himself that people (including psychotherapists) may not become as central to creative individuals as they are to the less gifted. The lessened centrality of persons as *objects* with its concomitant lessened centrality of interpersonal relatedness often earns the artist pejorative labels such as self-centered, infantile, or within the psychopathological lexicon, narcissistic.

Dylan Thomas' thoughts about poetry, particularly his early response to words and what they became for him, illustrate this special type of *object* relationship. Thomas writes:

> I wanted to write poetry in the beginning because I had fallen in love with words . . . what the words stood for, symbolized, or meant was of very secondary importance. What mattered was the *sound* of them as I heard them for the first time on the lips of the remote and incomprehensible grownups who seemed for some reason to be living in my world. . . . I fell in love—that is the only expression I can think of—at once and am still at the mercy of words, though sometimes now, knowing a little of their behavior very well, I think I can influence them slightly and have even learned to beat them now and then, which they appear to enjoy . . . when I began to read . . . I knew that I had discovered the most important things, to me, that could ever be. There they were, seemingly lifeless, made only of black and white, but out of them, out of their own being, came love and terror and pity and pain and wonder and all the vague abstractions that make our ephemeral lives dangerous, great, and bearable. . . . That was the time of innocence;

words burst upon me, unencumbered by trivial or portentous associations; words were their spring-like selves, fresh with Eden's dew as
they flew out of the air . . . [Thomas, 1951, pp. 147–148].

An observation by Joan Erikson (personal communication,
1982) of a potter's apology to a piece of work at a moment of
disappointment is a poignant illustration of an artist's "relating"
to his special type of *object*. Joan writes:

> Not too long ago, I witnessed an interesting demonstration. A fine potter
> was speaking to a group of craftspeople about his work. He had agreed
> to throw a pot for us, and we watched attentively as he centered the
> clay on the wheel and with expert skill began to mold and raise the
> form. . . . He turned the wheel, steadied his hands, and the clay stretched
> smoothly up and up. There was a good deal of tension in the audience,
> but not a word was spoken—only some breathy sounds of suspense
> were audible.
>
> As he finished off the rim with cautious fingers, the whole top
> collapsed and everyone groaned. The potter sighed. Then, he turned to
> us slowly and said, "Well, I guess I didn't give it my undivided atten-
> tion. I was too aware . . . of your expectations and just lost contact with
> the clay." Then, he gently touched the slumping pot and said, "Hey,
> I'm sorry"—not to us, but to the clay.

An example of this special type of *object* is found in the
remembrances of the then 18-year-old cello virtuoso, Matt Haimovitz (Ulrich, 1989). Haimovitz wrote, "When I heard the cello
for the first time I fell in love. . . . Since age 8, it has been the
love of [my] life. . . . [Sometimes] an instrument seems perfectly
fit for certain people. You can't imagine them playing anything
else. I'm attached to the cello" (pp. 34–39).

As a glimpse into how it feels to relate to a creative individual, we have the probably not overly accurate reminiscences of
Mozart's son, Carl. Listen to what it was like to take a walk in
the park with Mozart. Carl writes:

> "Now Carl," my father would say, "how about a walk in the park?"
> . . . And father would steer me out the door by my shoulder, and send
> me down the stairs, throwing my coat and hat on me as I descend-
> ed, . . . the dog skittering after me and father leaping down last.

I soon realized that our walks were conducted by father according to whatever tune was in his head. For dance music we generally stayed on the sides of roads and looked in people's windows. Father would gently push me before him, catch me and release me quietly by the waist, not quite partnering me, but guiding me in a melodious fashion. Airs and solos would stop him cold in the middle of the street, with his eyes open but not seeing, one hand opening and closing, little shakes of the head, lifts of the shoulders, a twitching knee.

He composed his overtures when the rest of the opera was complete, sometimes at the very last minute. Then it was hardly a walk, it was something more like headlong pursuit. I'd be chased up and down, I'd have to dodge people, dogs and carts, piles of refuse and excrement, and gaping holes of muddy water. Our terrier would be beside herself with excitement and fear. Horses would shy and merchants curse us. He wouldn't really see me in the course of these allegros, either, but he prodded me on mercilessly, whistling and humming, tugging my jacket, whacking my bottom, and I'd have to run so he wouldn't step on my heels.

At some point, I'd be running without him. He'd be back at the last corner with his notebook out, looking up only to find a place to crouch, something to lean against, or a surface to write on. Sometimes he'd borrow my back to write on. I'd have to stand with my hands on my knees until he cried "Got it." Then he'd wring my hands and straighten and kiss me, panting, "Thank-you, Carl, my boy, we are saved." Then he'd ask me what time it was and see if we couldn't buy ourselves a treat and some chocolate for mother [Poskitt, 1987–1988].

I suggest that the artist from early on relates to an expanded order of *object* that for some becomes a specific expressive composite of ideas and feelings organized and enacted as an entity loosely called "my art." "My art" largely parallels the *object* related expression "my love" referring to a person. Just as the dream is a common metaphor for expressing the subjective sense of the location of creativity, love is a common metaphor used by creative individuals to describe their relationship to their art. "My art" is commonly called "my first love," affirming that it comes first. From my perspective, "my first love" unwittingly reveals its developmental origins.

In describing origins, a common metaphor creative individuals use is that of "a gift," with the implication of its coming from without. The mythic representation of such visitations is the Muse, perhaps again betraying its origins as a woman.

This view of the importance of "a woman" in creativity is clearly described by Robert Graves (1948) when he discussed why many poets discontinue writing poetry. Rather than assigning the problem to " . . . the impossibility of earning a decent living by the profession of poetry," Graves writes, ". . . something dies in the poet. Perhaps he has compromised his poetic integrity by valuing some range of experience or other . . . above the poetic. But perhaps also he has lost his sense of White Goddess: the woman whom he took to be a Muse . . . " (p. 449).

As one would expect, just as in interpersonal relationships, the relationship with "my art" for most creative individuals is lifelong. Although easily romanticized by the less gifted, it is not an easy relationship, being as beset with jealousy, disappointment, feelings of abandonment, ecstatic union, replenishment, fulfillment, and a search for verification, as are interpersonal relationships for the less gifted.

Developmental Origins of Creativity

These speculations regarding the relationship of the artist to art add substantially to our understanding of the dynamics of creativity and open vistas for understanding the developmental origins and genesis of creativity. Although our knowledge regarding origins and genesis is rudimentary (in this respect, psychoanalysis is in good company) some beginnings do exist, particularly Winnicott's (1953) explorations of the part-me and part not-me aspect of the personality. In this metaphoric psychical *transitional space* Winnicott locates, to use his term, play, the dream, and creativity.

In Winnicott's speculations regarding the development of *object* relatedness, he notes a *transitional phase* during which the young child endows a connotative thing in the external world with psychological significance—the transitional *object*, traditionally a blanket. This endowing of a connotative thing becomes part of a process by which the early external presences—the composite of mothering functions and figures in the infant's life—become differentiated, integrated, and introjected as a concept, the mother, the internalized primal other. Viewed this way, the transitional *object* is the primal other one step removed as that other is being differentiated and integrated in the process of establishing internalized representations of self and nonself. In metapsychological terms, the process is the differentiation and integration of self and *object*. Stated in interpersonal terms, the process prototypically is differentiation of self from the mother that becomes integrated and generically self and other.

The transitional phase bridges monumental developmental epochs. The transitional period comprises the early experiencing of the external as part of an undifferentiated self/nonself matrix as it is transformed into differentiated, integrated concepts of self and *object*. The transitional phase is the beginning of separateness; it is ''continuity becoming contiguity,'' to use Winnicott's language. Contiguity demands communication and communication requires symbolization. The transitional phase, through a series of internal and internalizing events, coforms self and *object;* more accurately the transitional phase initiates the differentiation and integration of the self and *object* representations. Of colossal consequence, the separation of self and *object* representations enlivens symbolization. The human animal is becoming a human being.

Somewhat risking romanticism, this transitional process can be seen in reverse in the development of the art object. The sculptor inhales, eats, and is covered by the dust becoming one physically and psychologically as the stone becomes sculpture; similarly with paint and painter, as the paint becomes the painting.

Winnicott's concept of an ontogenetically evolving transitional space is of singular importance in the study of creativity in that it allows consideration of the developmental significance of connotative *things* endowed with meaning. Winnicott's view allows for speculation regarding the state and significance of the transitional space as it is influenced by the vicissitudes of the life of each individual. Winnicott's developmental considerations represent a new and substantial orientation in the psychoanalytic exploration of creativity. These considerations introduce a developmental complement adding to Freud's (1900, 1910, 1914) emphasis on mastery and resolution of conflict in motivating creativity. Winnicott's view easily accommodates Ernst Kris' (1952) emphasis on intrapsychic fluidity, Greenacre's (1957) "love affair with the world," and is close to but more developmentally specific than Heinz Kohut's (1966, 1971) reflections on creativity as a result of high-order self-integration.

Developmentally, creative people are those singular few individuals who maintain extraordinary continuances of transitional phenomena. As perpetuators of transitional phenomena, creative people continue the ongoing capacity to explore the external and the internal anew and to invent, play with, and enact symbols akin to the initial discovering we all experienced as the differentiation of self from nonself progressed. Such perpetuators are the creative beings whom we both cherish and treat badly, for through them we can, at times, vicariously reexperience the precious early excitement of initial discovery and the precious early excitement of forming novel and ever-varying symbols.

From this view, the transitional *object* and its institutional and psychopathological counterpart, the amulet and the fetish, are keystone developmental concepts for understanding the art object. Winnicott's emphasis on the transitional *object* closely parallels Emile Durkheim's (1915) description of the capacity to endow things with meaning as being the fundamental element of all religions. The capacity to endow things with meaning and to develop those meanings into integrated composites is the highest order of development of awareness. The ability to formalize and externalize these meaningful, integrated composites as symbols is creativity, the supreme achievement of evolution. Small wonder that John begins his history of the evolution of the God–humankind dialectic with, ''In the beginning was the Word, and the Word was with God, and the Word was God'' (John 1:1).

Pressing the developmental perspective, the transitional *object* links the art object and the religious object to the beginning of relatedness, a compelling parallel to the historical linkage between art and religion. Just as a historical commonality exists between the idol maker and the artist, a developmental commonality exists among the child playing, the idol maker, and the artist.

This emphasis on transitional experiencing leads us to consider creativity as a kind of relating to and communication rather than as mastery, as originally considered by Freud. From this *object*-related developmental view, the *that* of creativity, like the transitional *object*, is a transformation of the primal other. The *that* of creativity is a *who* who provides a protective presence for and a veritable matrix upon whom higher order enactment activities, including mastery enactments, are played out. *In short, creativity is a form of object relatedness.*

Object Relatedness, Sublimation, and Creativity

Joel Whitebook (1994), referring to Ricoeur (1970) and Castoriadis (1987), notes that a basic reason for a lack of an adequate theory of sublimation is that "the phenomenon cannot be satisfactorily accounted for on intrapsychic grounds alone, but must draw on extrapsychic, social reality as well" (p. 329). Whitebook, strongly inclined to energic concepts, needlessly limits his view of the relation between intrapsychic and social reality by not considering a third psychical field, the transitional field.

Although in psychoanalysis sublimation has always connoted transformations, originally of psychic energy and later of psychic contents, unfortunately in psychoanalysis sublimation also became associated with social acceptability.[3] Yet, social acceptance is of limited usefulness as a characteristic of creativity. In fact, creativity by virtue of its strong affinity to the original is far removed from social acceptability.

---

[3] Jung's concept *alchemy* as the study of transformations parallels Freud's concept *sublimation.* Using the word *alchemy* for psychic transformations somewhat betrays Jung's strong ties to mysticism and his enjoyment of being playfully shocking (Campbell, 1971).

Making social acceptability integral to sublimation confuses social acceptability of contents with social acceptability of mode. As Whitebook (1994) writes, sublimation is a "process through which genetic material, with all its contingency, privacy, and particularity, is transformed into cultural objects such as paintings, political constitutions, mathematical proofs, musical compositions, scientific theories . . . which can claim public validity in their respective domains" (p. 327). Whitebook, as would I, clearly distinguishes mode, the making of "cultural objects," from the content of those cultural objects.

By emphasizing the role of an internalized mediating *object*, sublimation differentiates itself from other defensive operations by freeing itself from the straitjacket of social acceptability.[4] Emphasizing the role of an internalized mediating *object* in sublimation meets the objections of Castoriadis (1987), Hans Loewald (1988), Ricoeur (1970), and Whitebook (1994) for the internalized mediating *object* is a representation, genetically specific, of extrapsychic, social reality, in the beginning personified by the mother.

Considering sublimation as a psychical transforming process involving an internal–external *object* in some ways places sublimation close to identification type defenses. Both are *object* involved, but sublimation, unlike identification, does not alter the internalizing agency, the hallmark of identification.

This *object*-related view of sublimation places sublimation distant from defense transformations related to simple manipulations of psychic contents, such as reaction formation, negation, and denial. Unlike reaction formation, negation, and denial, sublimation does not alter contents by transparently robbing them of their psychical values and psychical existence. Sublimation

---

[4] Defense in psychoanalysis originally described the variety of ways in which ideas and feelings are kept from awareness. The concept of defense, through increased understanding of the ego and superego, has come to mean the variety of ways ideas and feelings are altered, modified, and disguised to make them available to consciousness. Repetitive patterns of defensive constellations manifest as character and style.

through transformations modifies, enhances, and intensifies preserving psychical values by making external, multilevel communicating representations. From this point of view the archetypal image in sublimation is the magician transforming objects, the archaic priest. In ontogenetic terms, the internal–external mediating *object* is the mother of the transitional phase, the internal–external *object* who makes magical transformations of good into bad, bad into good, the unjust into the just, and the incomprehensible into the understandable.

This hierarchical view of transformations, somewhat borrowed from Otto Kernberg's (1968, 1975) view of hierarchical defenses, posits sublimation like identification as a high-order defense. Although sublimation is a high level of defense, it becomes a different order of transformation by virtue of its externalizing capacity. Identification makes for internal creations, highly limited by the nature of the relationship to the internalized *object* and its characteristics. Sublimation allows for external, nearly limitless creation. *Identifications change the personality; sublimations change the world.*

Positing sublimation as a transformational process of a different order further frees creativity from psychopathological formulations and enlightens the mythical links between creativity, magic, dreams, and the divine. Of more importance, this view of sublimation provides a developmental window for studying these "magical syntheses," to use Silvano Arieti's (1976) propitious phrase.

The Patron

The patron is the unsung hero in creativity. There are important heuristic reasons to differentiate the patron as person and the patron as intrapsychic concept. The patron as intrapsychic concept is an essential component in the psychodynamics of creativity.

Even though the form of the patron changes through epochs, I suggest that there is always a patron as concept for the creative person. In the Renaissance, the patron was personified in the powerful prince, nobleman, cardinal, or pope. Lorenzo the Magnificent and the "Medici Garden," which was an invention of Georgio Vasari, have been romanticized to near mythic stature (Chamberlin, 1982). As patron, Lorenzo has become allegorical. In the nineteenth century the patron was often a particular kind of woman, for example, the Austrian painter Egon Schiele's Wally. Today the patron is frequently an institution, a university, or a government agency.

Viewed ontogenetically, creativity is a high level of transitional functioning, which characteristically operates under the aegis of an "other." This primal other is reactualized in the patron. Like the mother for the developing infant, the concept of patron is closely related to the "transitional field" in which the creative person explores with a sense of safety.

The patron as concept, like the transitional mother, by being a part of what the infant is exploring (the transitional *object*) safeguards the creative person as the creative person explores a "new" external world. Both patron and mother provide the potential for return to a state of safe oneness. The patron is an actualized reaffirmation of the internalized primal other protecting the creative person from the utter aloneness of exploration. The patron provides the feeling of "safe return," ameliorating the many perils internal and external in the exploration of the new.

In psychodynamic terms, the patron protects the creative individual from the *objectlessness* that is part of being original. In short, creativity is freighted with the dread of utter aloneness and the patron, to a varying extent, is an ameliorating *object*. The patron is the avatar of the protecting mother.[5] In a way

---

[5] In the lives of both the talented and the creative there are important others who note, foster, and protect the unusual abilities and the individual. However, psychodynamically patron functioning is markedly different from the mentor, the provider of identifications, in talent as detailed in chapter 4, "Talent and Creativity."

reminiscent of Theo van Gogh, note how protectively, sensitively, and I would add maternally Sanford Pollock in 1941 wrote of his brother during a particularly bleak period for Jackson. "Jackson's art . . . will, I am convinced, come to great importance . . . we are sure that if he is able to hold himself together his work will become of real significance. His painting is abstract, intense, evocative . . . " (Wysuph, 1970).

Recognizing the transitional functioning of the patron does not mean that the patron as person does not affect creativity. At times, the patron as person is patently manifest in the content of the art. The complex and perilous relation among patron, model, lover, and artist is particularly evident in Picasso (MacGregor-Hastie, 1988; Richardson, 1991).

At times, the patron as person may interfere with creativity or inhibit it completely. The patron, jealous of, at times frightened by, the creative person's absorption in "the art" may attempt, sometimes successfully, to eliminate "the art."[6] The parallel is easily drawn to the mother who interferes with or even completely inhibits transitional progressions in her child. The interference by the mother may reflect her conscious and unconscious competition with and/or fear of any *object* other than herself in the child's life or newness in general.

Edward

As an example of a mother's fear of her child's creativity, some years ago, I was consulted by a physicist, Edward, who was very lonely and depressed. Highly esteemed by colleagues and widely regarded as headed for a Nobel Prize, Edward complained that he quickly lost interest in people and they with him.

---

[6] The jealousy of the creative person's absorption in "the art" was beautifully described by Robert Graves (1948) in his discussion of why young poets stop writing poetry. Graves writes, " . . . the woman . . . who was his Muse turns into a domestic woman and would have him turn similarly into a domesticated man. Loyalty prevents him from parting company with her, especially if she is the mother of his children" (p. 449).

Edward's unusual intelligence and quick grasp of configurations interfered with relationships. For example, going to a movie with a friend easily became a social disaster. At a movie, Edward typically quickly grasped the structure of the story and the movie lost interest for him. Early in the film, he would exasperate his companion by explaining how the plot was to unfold and want to leave. Going to a movie with a friend epitomized his dilemma. Although he wanted to ''be close'' to people, he always was far ahead of them.

Edward was reared in a small Midwestern town, the only child of rather ordinary people. His father ran a store and his mother worked in it. When Edward was in the fourth grade, the science teacher suggested that each child develop a science project. Edward began tinkering with electricity and with various devices. His mother was frightened by his activities and the intensity of his involvement. She told him that he should go outside and play with friends.

Edward continued working on his device often late into the night. The mother feared that he was ruining his ''health'' and that his playing with electricity was dangerous. One time about 2 A.M. she found him in the garage secretly working on his ''device.'' She cried out, ''You are going to drive yourself crazy'' and smashed the apparatus. He clandestinely continued developing his project.

One day, the science teacher called the parents to school. The teacher explained that he had assigned science projects to the class. Most of the students bought simple kits to assemble, such as kits of the human body or of dinosaurs. The teacher was sure that Edward had made a rudimentary computer. He said that he wanted to send Edward's project to the local university for confirmation. The mother was immensely relieved. Silently she had feared that her son had become ''some sort of a mad scientist.''[7] The advanced nature of what the boy had created was

---

[7] Recognizing the importance of regression with dedifferentiation of self and *object* in the psychodynamics of creativity helps explain the linkage in the popular mind, literature, and in mythology between creativity and madness.

easily confirmed and he was enrolled in a special program for gifted children at the university. He received his Ph.D. in physics when he was 15.

Discussion. Edward illustrates the importance of the patron (teacher) in recognizing, fostering, and protecting creativity. He also well illustrates the patron (mother) gone awry. The mother feared what she thought was *objectlessness* (madness) in her son's activity. She tried to "normalize" him (make him more interpersonally related) by sending him out to play with other children. As her fears mounted, to protect him she smashed the device which she saw as consuming him.

The teacher, recognizing that the boy's project reflected originality and not idiosyncrasy, was able to explain to the parents the extraordinary circumstance in which they found themselves. He made sense out of the boy's behavior and the device saving both from catastrophe. Yet, today, Edward goes from "patron" to "patron" in search of someone who can tolerate the extraordinary rapidity with which he evaluates configurations and which thrusts him far ahead and therefore alone in almost any circumstance.

Freud–Fliess–Jung

In the history of psychoanalysis, extraordinary documentation of this patron function exists in the Fliess–Freud relationship (Freud, 1897–1902). Wilhelm Fliess, an older physician and specialist in diseases of the nose, throat, and ears, lived in Berlin. Fliess had many idiosyncratic ideas about the relationship between the nose and sexual problems. That Freud idealized Fliess and his peculiar notions is one of the mysteries of psychoanalysis.

Via letters, Fliess was Freud's earliest confidant. During these years, Freud revealed to Fliess some of his most important psychological discoveries. A perusal of Fliess' correspondence suggests that Fliess, whom we now know was psychotic, rarely responded directly to Freud's revelations or questions about them. Indeed it seems that Fliess' autistic preoccupations kept him from understanding and, therefore, from interfering with Freud's development. Fliess provided Freud with an idea of being understood, not the actuality.

This relationship stands in marked contrast to another of Freud's early psychoanalytic associations of vast importance, his relationship with Jung. Carl G. Jung, a brilliant young psychiatrist in Zurich, initially became for Freud his heir apparent. In the Jung–Freud correspondence, Jung clearly understood what Freud presented and attempted to discuss and alter it (McGuire, 1974). Theirs was a true *object* relatedness with all the vicissitudes of intergenerational competitive conflict. This inevitably led to a breach allowing each great mind to pursue its originality. In the interactions among Freud, Fliess, and Jung, we see played out almost allegorically the difference between patron functioning (Fliess) and interpersonal impingement (Jung) on creativity (Freud).

Julius II–Michelangelo

Among the interesting and compelling patron–artist relationships was that of Pope Julius II and Michelangelo. Julius as person often impinged on Michelangelo's creativity. At times Julius interfered because affairs of state distracted him and at times because he ran out of money. Often he interfered with Michelangelo's creativity by moving Michelangelo from project to project for self-serving reasons.

The "tragedy," as Michelangelo called it, of the Tomb for Julius II has been studied by numerous art historical and psychoanalytic scholars (Panofsky, 1939; Tolnay, 1970; Hibbard, 1974; Liebert, 1982). Most likely the Tomb failed because it was an impossible task reflecting a megalomaniacal fantasy shared by these two great men. They planned to outdo the myth of what

Mausolus created at Halicarnassus. Yet out of that aborted super-human effort came a more attainable but nonetheless superhuman project and an intense interpersonal drama, the decoration of the ceiling of the Sistine Chapel.

Despite the turmoil that Julius created, we must consider that he "protected" Michelangelo from their shared megalomania by "pulling him off" the impossible Tomb project and insisting on his working on the more possible ceiling project. All that we know about Julius indicates that such "protection" was highly self-serving. Yet, we must consider that beneath the conflicted, intergenerational, father–son relationship that dominated the Michelangelo–Julius dyad, paradoxically, Julius as patron "conceived" and "allowed" the ceiling to come into being. In short, as a multilayered composite, Julius as patron participated in Michelangelo's creativity as a conducive presexual, maternal fundament, a patron, while Julius as person caused Michelangelo inordinate misery and frustration and deprived history of many masterpieces.

The "Unseen" Audience

More fundamental and complex than the patron in the psychodynamics of creativity is the "unseen" audience. Universally, but with varying degrees of explicitness, creative individuals sense that creativity involves a kind of dialogue with the art object.[8] This externally enacted sense of dialogue is a manifestation of an "out there and yet inside" dialogue. The dialogue is compound in that it is a "conversation" with and at the same time about the *object*. Developmentally, this dialogue with the *object* and with the "unseen" audience recapitulates the relationship of the transitional phase. The dialogue is with the *object*, the

---

[8] This dialogue with the art object is recapitulated in art appreciation. As detailed in chapter 3, "Dream Interpretation and Art Appreciation," what seems an inner monologue between the viewer and the art piece is in fact a complex dialogue between the viewer and the artist.

mother one step removed, and with the ''unseen'' audience, also the mother.

For performers the situation is further complicated. In addition to the ''unseen'' audience, there is the actual audience. Performers sense the presence of the audience and its effect on their performing. At times they are aware of entering into a dialogue with the audience, these being regarded as some of their most creative moments.

The critic in a way is a personification of the ''unseen'' audience. Although most artists, including performers, minimize the effect of the critics as person and as concept on their art, my experience with artists suggests that most if not all artists, particularly performers, are highly aware of and heavily influenced by the critic as concept and to a great extent as person. Many are aware of a constant fear of the critic and know how inhibiting this fear can be.

The Primal Other and Creativity

This emphasis on the role of the mother in creativity parallels Lewin's (1953) schematic view of the dream as being ''upon'' the dream screen and Erikson's understanding of child's play (1937, 1954, 1977). As noted in chapter 2, ''The Dream, Art, and Psychoanalysis,'' it is difficult with brevity to epitomize Lewin's and Erikson's concepts. Independently Erikson and Lewin saw the mother as an underlying continuing presence in the dream of the adult and in the play of children. Lewin, using the cinema screen as an analogy, conceptualized the mother's body as an invisible continuing presence, ''the screen,'' hidden beneath but upon which the dream is experienced. Erikson saw the ''location'' of play as that same invisible continuing presence. In essence, the child and his or her play and the dreamer in his or her dreams nightly bring the day's experiences, the joys and the disappointments, intermixed with the unconscious past, to the mother to enjoy the "good," make right the "bad," make the unjust just and the incomprehensible understandable.

Unlike Lewin, who emphasized the physicality of the mother's breast and body as the organizing external presences, the dream screen, I emphasize the importance of the responding mother's face oriented by the gleam of the eyes. To me the responding face is affectful reacting to asymmetries within a basic essential symmetry.

With development, this basic orienting principle, symmetry, is reenforced by the kinesthetic explorations of the symmetry of one's own body. The template for expressing and evaluating emotions continues with the body's, especially the face's, basic symmetry. Nowhere is the affectful potential of the face's and body's symmetry as template more profitably exploited than in abstract art and dance.

The Process of Creating

The creative object, like the early transitional *object,* is part self and part other and yet separate from both self and other. When studied closely, creativity recapitulates the major developmental levels of ontogenesis. The process of the development of the creative object recapitulates primary fusion emerging into differentiation.

The "moments" of inspiration seem subjectively close to the regressive dedifferentiation of self and *object* that progresses into transitional differentiation. During the regressive dedifferentiation of self and *object* there is often dedifferentiation of the sensory modalities as sound, sight, and kinesthetic qualities blend. Beethoven once wrote:

> I carry my thoughts about with me for a long time, often for a very long time before writing them down. I can . . . be sure that . . . I shall not forget (a theme) even years later. I change many things, discard others, and try again and again until I am satisfied; then, in my head, I begin to elaborate the work . . . the underlying idea never deserts me.

It rises, it grows. I hear and see the image in front of me from every angle [Hamburger, 1952, p. 194; emphasis added].

The great jazz artist John Birks (Dizzy) Gillespie in an interview stated:

The hardest part of music is improvising, and it gets harder the older you are. Improvisation is a gathering together of all the evidence you have of how to resolve going from here to here to here. It's similar to painting. You add colors in your mind, you build colors. Bright yellow is generally loud, green is soft. I'm a more melodious player then I used to be, but rhythm is still my business. I see rhythm when I play, I understand rhythm, my best shot is rhythm. Harmony is next [Balliet, 1990, p. 48].

The inspirational quality characterizing creative thinking in government and business is well documented in Franklin Roosevelt's response to Winston Churchill's 1941 desperate wartime plea that, "The moment approaches when we shall no longer be able to pay cash for shipping and other supplies." Doris Goodwin (1994) writes:

Churchill's letter had a profound effect on the President, but he said little about it at first. "I didn't know for quite awhile what he was thinking about, if anything," Harry Hopkins said later, "I began to get the idea that he was refuelling, the way he so often does when he seems to be resting and carefree. So I didn't ask him any questions. Then one evening, he suddenly came out with it—the whole program. He didn't seem to have any clear idea how it could be done legally. But there wasn't a doubt in his mind that he'd find a way to do it." The *whole program*, later was known as *lend-lease*. . . . How Roosevelt arrived at this ingenious idea, which cut through all the old debates in Washington about loans and gifts is not clear. "Nobody that I know of," Robert Sherwood wrote, "has been able to give any convincing idea" of how the refuelling process worked. "He did not seem to talk much about the subject in hand, or to consult the advice of others, or to read-up on it. . . . One can only say that FDR, *a creative artist in politics*, had put in his time . . . evolving the pattern of a masterpiece" (emphasis added).[9] Frances Perkins later described the President as having "flashes of

---

[9] It is interesting that Sherwood uses the word *artist* and *masterpiece* as I do. The artists are the creative few transcending field.

almost clairvoyant knowledge and understanding." He would have one of these flashes every now and then, she observed, much like the ones that musicians get when "they see or hear the structure of an entire symphony or opera." He couldn't always hold on to it or verbalize it, but when it came he suddenly understood how all kinds of disparate things fitted together. While Henry Stinson, the Secretary of War, could justly complain that trying to follow the President's intuitive thought processes as he moved from one idea to the next in no logical order was "very much like chasing a vagrant beam of sunshine around a vacant room," the President made up for the defects of an undisciplined mind with a profound ability to integrate a vast multitude of details into a large pattern, which gave shape and direction to the stream of events [p. 46].

Just as the primary dedifferentiations give way to transitional experiencing, transitional experiencing gives way to a differentiated tertiary process as the object on a more cognitive level is worked on, over, and with relating it to and making it an extension of its genre. Only then does it become the art piece. Developmentally, creativity is a recapitulated progression and intermixing of infantile, childlike, and adult functioning.

It is creativity's intimacy with the threshold between primary fusion and differentiation that links and distinguishes creativity from mystical experience and it should be added, madness. In contrast to the creative individual, the mystic seeks the dedifferentiation of self and nonself. The mystic seeks self–nonself merger. The mystical state attempts to establish the "oceanic" feeling paralleling the earliest developmental period of primary fusion obliterating the need for communication. Creativity, paralleling the transitional period, reestablishes an emerging differentiation of self and nonself coforming the need for communication.

The mystic attempts to achieve a state and can only instruct others in how to achieve a like state. The creative person plays with experiences and attempts to communicate experience, new and familiar, in new ways. The self-absorption in self and *object* merger and transitional functioning links creativity to madness.

Creating viewed this way is a reestablishing of primal union at a variety of levels with the primal *object* out of which a new object comes into being (Winnicott, 1967; Oremland, 1984). Like *object* relatedness, creativity seeks a version of the primal *object* out of which evolves the creation of a new object that is a version of the primal *object*. In the interpersonal realm, the parallel to the child begs to be drawn. Both creativity and *object* relatedness establish continuities and continuing.

Art, *Object,* and Personal Continuity

As important as art is for the artist as a source of expression, replenishment, self-validation, and self-realization, such imperatives pale before a more fundamental purpose—art's promise of personal continuity. Continuing the parallel to *object* relatedness, creativity, like *object* relatedness, potentially provides personal continuity—immortality through issue.

Warding off the fear of finiteness is a fundamental motivation for *object* relatedness and for working. Our capacity to relate and be related to allows us to be carried psychologically within (incorporated by) another—to be continued within the person and within the issue of the relationship.

Work, also, provides the potential for personal continuity. One's work can continue after one is gone. It is as though a psychoanalytically oriented Providence, with a greater wisdom that personal continuity not be dependent solely on interpersonal relatedness, provides two pathways toward immortality—love and work. From this vantage point, Freud's alleged definition of mental health as the capacity to love and work fully takes on rich meaning. Although rarely acknowledged, psychoanalysis is as much a psychology of continuity as it is a psychology of drives.

Creativity can provide a literal immortality. Indeed, part of our ambivalence toward creative individuals, why we are in awe of them and treat them poorly, reflects our envious awareness that among them stand the immortals.

Summary

The investigation of the relationship of the artist to his art is a study of the origin of the creative matrix upon which higher order defensive activities are enacted as forms, themes, and narratives. Freud began with the study of external expression in forms, themes, and narratives as the mastery of trauma, delving later through his exploration of the dream into the formation and structure of the art object, itself.

Through the study of the place of the *that* in ontogenesis, we are beginning to understand the origins of creativity as being rooted, as it were, in the coforming of self and the personal and impersonal nonself, the external objects endowed with connotative meaning. It is the continual exploring and rediscovering of the internal and external worlds anew and the playing with and evolving novel symbols that characterize the transitional phase that are the stuff of art.

6

Creativity and Sexuality

Homosexuality and Creativity

It seems unlikely that we will ever know if there is an integral affinity between homosexuality and creativity. Even though we seem to be moving into an enlightened view of homosexuality with increasing willingness by individuals to identify themselves as being homosexual, because of the great difficulty in defining homosexuality and the great difficulty in defining creativity we are a long way from establishing whether creative individuals more than others tend toward, choose, or are driven toward homosexuality. Yet, as acquired immunodeficiency syndrome (AIDS) related illnesses and deaths have robbed individuals, particularly creative individuals and celebrities, of the opportunity to choose whether or not to identify themselves as homosexuals, one is impressed by what seems to be a higher than expected correlation between homosexuality and creativity. The issue is further complicated because of the wide range of manifestations of creativity and of homosexuality. Is homosexuality more related to certain kinds of creativity? Is it only a matter of visibility that homosexuality seems more frequent in men associated with dance and the theater than those involved with painting, writing, and sculpture?

Homosexuality is the complex result of an interrelation of physical traits, identifications, and object choice. Strictly speaking homosexuality should be defined as same-sex object choice. Yet there are difficulties in differentiating certain kinds of narcissistic object choice from choice of objects of the same sex. Further, various kinds of homosexuality, like heterosexuality, may be more a matter of perversion than object relatedness. It must also be acknowledged that as unclear as is our understanding of male homosexuality, our understanding of female homosexuality, like our understanding of female heterosexuality, is even further from complete.

Hermaphroditism, Biunity, and Creativity

Psychoanalysis is indebted to Kris (1952) for freeing our understanding of creativity from psychopathology. Kris understood that the fluidity in intrapsychic structuring with accessibility to unconscious mental processes that is essential for creativity should not be confused with looseness of intrapsychic structuring and uncontrolled invasion by unconscious mental processes characteristic of certain kinds of psychopathology.

Expanding on Kris, I propose that the flexibility in intrapsychic structuring characteristic of creativity often is associated with a fluid sense of maleness and femaleness that should not be constricted by the conventional gender-defining words *masculine* and *feminine*. I suggest that the subjective sense of shifting maleness and femaleness in the creative person is at times loosely and erroneously considered homosexuality by the creative person and others and at times may be enacted in a variety of relationships, often perverse, that loosely appear homosexual. This shifting sense of maleness and femaleness is readily identifiable in the lives and art of Michelangelo and of Leonardo, and this tendency toward enactment helps explain the curious maternal masochistic intensity that marked their relationships with beautiful boys, particularly Michelangelo's idealized love of Cecchino and Leonardo's worship of Salai, "the little Satan."

Exploring this shifting sense of masculinity and femininity in creativity reveals that gender fluidity is but a manifestation and a component of developmentally early, in that sense primitive, fantasies of hermaphroditism, autoinsemination, and autogestation that are fundaments in creativity. Such epicene fantasies, a kind of primal *biunity*, have long been closely associated with creativity in mythology. A noteworthy example is found in the Hindu idiom, the overtly hermaphroditic form of Shiva, the *Ardhanarisvara* (twelfth century) (Figure 11). As the "lord who is half-female," this manifestation of Shiva is closely associated with, to quote Stella Kramrisch, "creating, the embodiment of the ultimate source from which unfolds the observable world *out of his own substance*" (1981; emphasis added).

As an illustration of this primal biunity, I offered (1989) Michelangelo's provocative, enigmatic, complex Leda image in his now lost *Leda and the Swan* (1531) (Figure 12). If the Bos rendition is accurate, as most Michelangelo scholars believe, it contains an autoerotic, hermaphroditic autoinsemination structure in its latently homoerotic theme. I read the central figure, the Leda, not only as a phallicized and masculinized female with specific developmental and defensive implications, but more importantly as limning self-fellatio and oral self-insemination. The hermaphroditic Leda represents primal oneness, a primitive *biunity*. The fertilized egg, continuing this line of thought, symbolizes the parthenogenic self-conception; for the artist, it is the art object, itself.

Carrying this idea further, it is in the Sistine ceiling's *Histories* (1508–1512) that Michelangelo overtly addresses a pictorialization of creation. As Michelangelo makes visible the transformation of the Divine into humankind, the breasted androgynic God in *Separation of Light from Darkness* (Figure 13) transmutes altar to entrance wall into the highly gender-defined and procreative Noah's family worshiping Him, *Sacrifice of Noah* (Figure 14). Before our eyes, primal creativity transmutes into human generativity. In Michelangelo's hands the Old Testament's account of the descent of man becomes the "ascent" of

FIGURE 11.   *Ardhanarisvara*, Chola Dynasty (Twelfth century).
(Courtesy of Stella Kramrisch.)

FIGURE 12. *Leda and the Swan*, Michelangelo (Bos copy) (1531). (Courtesy of the Trustees of the British Museum, London.)

FIGURE 13.   *Separation of Light from Darkness*, Michelangelo
(1508–1512). (Courtesy of the Monumenti Musei e Gallerie Pontificie,
The Vatican.)

humankind. Michelangelo's development of humankind from the
Divine is a metaphor for ontogenesis. In Michelangelo's "ascent," as in ontogenesis, creativity becomes human generativity.

It is in hermaphroditic imagery, which reaches an artistic
apogee in certain works of Michelangelo (1508–1512) (Figure
15) and Leonardo (1515) (Figure 2), that we find the biunity,
even the nascent creativity, in our primal selves. Michelangelo's
and Leonardo's hermaphroditic images allow us to reexperience
primal unity with its miraculous sense of creative omnipotence.

Figure 14.   *Sacrifice of Noah*, Michelangelo (1508–1512). (Courtesy of the Monumenti Musei e Gallerie Pontificie, The Vatican.)

No wonder their hermaphroditic images transcend culture and
epoch and are endlessly interesting, at times disturbing, to countless tens of thousands.

At the risk of being overly sweeping, I suggest that as gender differentiation prevails generativity becomes the primary, for

FIGURE 15.   *Ignudi,* Michelangelo (1508–1512). (Courtesy of the
Monumenti Musei e Gallerie Pontificie, The Vatican.)

most, the sole continuation of primal creativity.[1] Creativity and procreating are one but on vastly different psychical levels. Creativity at base is a reestablishing of primal biunity with the primal object, the mother, out of which a new object comes into being. Like object relatedness, creativity seeks a version of the primal object out of which evolves the creation of a new object that is a version of the primal object.

Stated another way, creativity is a "parthenogenic" version of object-related generativity. Both are intensely motivated by object seeking and both potentially provide personal perpetuity through issue. The *oeuvre* of the artist is as crucial to the artist's continuance as is the child for the artist's "object-related" cohort. The art object like the child is simultaneously the past (the primal object), the present (the self), and the future (an amalgam of both). Creativity, like generativity, potentially assures continuities and both are primarily motivated by the desire for psychological immortality. As Erikson (1954) wrote:

> [T]he creative individual's typical cycle of moods and attitudes . . . probably permits him, at the height of consummation, to identify with father, mother, and newborn child, all in one; to represent in equal measure, his father's potency, his mother's fertility, and his own reborn ideal identity. It is obvious, then why mankind participates, with pity and terror, with ambivalent admiration and ill-concealed abhorrence in the hubris of creative men, and why such hubris, in these men themselves, can call forth all the sinister forces of . . . conflict [p. 49].

Women, Children, and Creativity

Discussing the relation of creativity to procreation raises perplexing and potentially unanswerable questions regarding the relation of women to creativity. The list of creative women,

---

[1] The "perils" of generativity to creativity are fully alluded to by Robert Graves (1948) when he discusses poets' failing to continue writing. "Perhaps The White Goddess: the woman . . . who was a muse turns into a domestic woman and would have him turn similarly into a domesticated man. The White Goddess is anti-domestic; she is the perpetual 'other woman,' and her part is difficult indeed for a woman . . . to

although impressive, is markedly short when compared with that of creative men. It was frequently voiced in and outside psychoanalysis that women find their creativity in pregnancy, parturition, and child rearing and therefore do not need or seek other channels for creative expression. In psychoanalysis at one time it was even fashionable to consider that men's creativity primarily rose out of jealousy of women's ability to have children. Although these weak theories are from the period when creativity was seen as defensive compensation, I would not minimize men's jealousy of women's ability to make a child as a motivation in creativity. There is reason to suspect that Picasso's psychological and physical maltreatment and abandonment of his many women lovers and wives when they became pregnant was a representation of his envy of their ability to make a child. Even though he was one of the most creative men of all time, it seems that it galled him that women could easily create what he never could, a living being (MacGregor-Hastie, 1988; Stassinopoulos, 1988; Richardson, 1991; Gilot, 1964).

The current highly subscribed view regarding women and creativity in and outside psychoanalysis is that through the ages women for a variety of socioeconomic reasons have been systematically deprived of opportunities to be creative. Related to this idea is that there are and always have been strong societal forces, conscious and unconscious, limiting women, relegating them to the role of assistants to men, be they wives, mistresses, or patrons with regard to creativity.

Embedded in these polarizations of nature–nurture issues are implications regarding the need of men and women to procreate. More important are the implications of the differences in the meaning to men and women of having children.

My experience with creative women is, as one would expect, less than with men, but nonetheless substantial in terms of

---

play for more than a few years'' (p. 449). It is not known what Graves thought regarding creativity in women, but he clearly noted the perils to creative men of heterosexual interpersonal relatedness (as opposed to transitional ''patron'' functioning) when he wrote, ''the temptation to commit suicide in simple domesticity lurks in every maenad's and muse's heart'' (p. 449).

depth and intensity. In talking with creative women about their work and their children, it is striking that creative women talk about their children much the way men do. In contrast creative women tend to talk about their creativity and what they create the way women talk about their children. I have noticed generally that creative men talk about their creativity and what they create the way women talk about their children, and they talk about their children much the way other men do.

This is not to say that creative and noncreative men and creative women are not interested in their children but rarely does having a child have the centrality to their self-concept that having a child has for noncreative women.[2]

If these observations are generalizable, we can begin to understand the greater difficulty creative women have in serving their many physiological, psychological, and social masters. Yet, the difficulties should not be seen simply as competing interests. The productively creative women whom I know in depth confess that they are not torn between their creativity and children. Although most sense varying degrees of remorse, in their heart of hearts the creativity always came first. Even though all creative women experience enormous internal and external expectations regarding having and rearing children, for some the expectations are so great that their creativity permanently succumbs to it. Almost universally, when the creativity was intensely inhibited by their conscience about having or being with their children, there was marked depression with, at the very least, ambivalence toward their children, their husbands, and their lives. The women who were successful as mothers and creative individuals frequently confessed that essentially their mothers, rarely their husbands, raised the children.

I have had experience with adult children of creative people that corroborates these observations. There were striking differences between the way children of creative men and women

---

[2] There are highly developed psychoanalytic speculations many of which are controversial regarding the psychical centrality of having a child to women. These speculations related to ideas about completion of body image, fantasies regarding the

reacted to their parents' creativity. Rarely do the children of creative men have the intensity of ambivalence or outright anger toward their creative fathers that the children of creative mothers have toward their mothers. Although the children of creative fathers complained about the father's preoccupation and lack of emotional availability, they turned to their mothers whom they often recognized, with some antagonism and jealousy, protected the father and his creativity. Largely these children came to appreciate and cherish their fathers and their fathers' art. This is not to say that these families were continually in a state of equilibrium. Often there was anger, mistrust, resentment, and divorce. When there was divorce, in no case did the creative father keep the children, although often the relation with the children improved after the divorce when the children were involved in a more scheduled and limited way with the father.

The children of creative women strongly complained about their mother's creativity.[3] Until they were adults and sometimes only when they were in psychotherapy did the children of creative mothers identify the competition with their mother's creativity. The mother's creativity was always a part of their lives. As the competition was recognized, they realized that from the beginning they knew that it was a competition they could never win. The rare cases in which the child was actually abandoned by the creative mother and lived separately with the father or grandparents, the child had nearly unrelenting hostility toward the mother and her creativity.

As would be anticipated, if creativity is integral with transitional functioning, the fundamentals of creativity are established prior to gender differentiation with a preoedipal, highly dyadic, maternal orientation. Although I fear being misconstrued as reviving the pathological cast on creativity that characterized early

_____

father's penis, and essential identifications with mother and mothering, are intrinsic to the psychoanalytic concepts of femininity, being female, and motherhood.

[3] One woman, daughter of a concert violinist, referred to herself as the "second fiddle," completely unaware of the literal accuracy of the metaphor. As a child she was painfully aware of the intensity of her hatred for her mother's violin. It was not until psychoanalysis that she recognized that the ambivalence was toward her mother.

psychoanalytic writings and that I have been struggling to overthrow, the pregender roots of creativity seem clear and suggest that neither gender has a hegemony.

Yet, it seems that it might be easier for males to maintain the quest for the transitional maternal object. The male developmental line is characterized by maintaining the primary object with the nature of the bond changing, whereas the female developmental line is more complex and potentially conflicted. Female development demands that not only the nature of the bond be changed and that the primary object be abandoned, but that the primary object be replaced by a new object. Said more simply, in heterosexual development, the male maintains an ongoing tie to the mother, and later the wife, the mother once removed. The female comes into conflict with the mother over the possession of the father. The little girl must to a large measure abandon essential ties to the mother and replace her with a new object, the father.

From this standpoint, it seems that psychology and its institutionalized external representations, society, for both sexes conspire against creativity in favor of procreation, but this is particularly so for female creativity. Here we step deeply into complex and only recently explored areas regarding essential differences in the genesis of the male and female, the societal response to and direction thereof, and the place of the desire to have a child in development.

7

Responses

A Painter Responds

Françoise Gilot

In Europe when I was younger, artists lived in terror of Freudian analysts. We thought that the net result of psychoanalysis was to deprive one of the ability to create, a high price to pay for release from anxiety. Of course, often there were friendships between psychoanalysts and artists. I and other painters were friends with Drs. Jacques Lacan, Serge Liebovici, René Diadkine, and Cornelius Castoriadis. They were always amused that we were adamant about refusing to be analyzed by any of them on the grounds that we did not want to loose our acumen as painters. All this is to say that great progress has been made during the last thirty years and Jerome Oremland's work furthers that progress.

Not being a psychoanalyst, it is not necessary for me to comment much on the first three chapters, except to say that it is helpful to remove creativity from the realm of psychopathology and articulating relevant analogies between the *dream period* in sleep and in wakefulness and the natural unfolding of the

Painter, writer, and poet, Mme. Gilot was awarded the Commander dans L'Order des Arts et Lettres in 1988 and the Chevalier de la Legion d'Honneur in 1990.

creative spirit. Of course, Marcel Proust repeatedly said to friends, including the author and philosopher Emmanuel Berl and Pablo Picasso, who later quoted him to me: "There is no art without neurosis." Proust probably meant that inner conflicts increase the pressure necessary to focus and concentrate. Perhaps conflicts enhance the power to symbolize, the indomitable surge from suppression and repression to the liberation of expression.

It was thrilling to see the distinction Oremland makes between talent and creativity. As he rightly indicates *talent* pertains to skills, to knowledge, and to all that can be learned which will enhance the inner drive if both are consonant. Separate is the essential factor, the factor Oremland calls *creativity*. Yet, how can we define creativity if not by examining the works of art taken in a broad sense, including science, that stand as proofs to its existence? Is not creativity an overwhelming desire, an imperative, and a promise that can only be fulfilled by its realization in a specific medium? Creativity is not a *desire to do*, it is a desire *to be* and *to become*. What are the components of such a compelling compulsion? In what proportions do the genetic, the sociological, and cultural elements concur to its manifestation?

There are, of course, family clusters in the arts like the Casadesus in music, the Tiepolos and the Breughels in painting, and the Brontë sisters in writing. The privilege of good connections between brain, ear, eye, limbs, and hands may be innate, but the influences from nurture provide channels that facilitate an as yet incoherent desire.

It may take more than one generation of capable, talented people to produce a great artist. Did Leopold Mozart bully his son into becoming a genius? That is not possible! Or was not Leopold just lucky that little Wolfgang had what it took to soar above everyone else? Picasso's father was a good painter, not a great painter, but he was his son's mentor and that became his greatest achievement. There are also dynasties of great bankers like the Rothschilds. It is as if latent tendencies can develop as actual aspirations and be realized only through time. A specific talent already considered acceptable or commonplace in a given family can be of help to the creative individual because it assuages the terror of revelations resulting from the exploration of the inner self. Talent is like a mask that helps to conceal genius as long as the artist has not built enough self-confidence for total disclosure of who he or she really is and no longer cares if what he or she expresses is acceptable or not. As Oremland writes, talent can be a defense against the anxieties of being creative.

In common parlance, a work of art is an object, but this is a difficult concept for the artist to entertain, at least as far as one's work is concerned. I offer the following metaphor. If a person walks on the wet sand of a beach, the purpose is to go from one end to the other. In so doing footprints are left behind as an objective proof of the action taken. Are the footprints objects? In the same way works of art are traces of an artist's quest. They are objective clues, but are they objects? They become objects as they are beheld, heard, appreciated, or rejected by others. I believe Oremland writes well about the process of artistic inspiration *and* art appreciation. Different minds, different sensibilities reenact the creative phase in themselves through assimilation or rejection.

I recognize that Oremland uses the word *object* in two ways. *Object* defined psychoanalytically and object as the product of creativity, the art object. I believe that when Oremland talks about the art object as a creation part self and part other and yet separate from both, he is close to the way I think of the art piece.

This leads me to Oremland's concept of the "masterpiece" that I find interesting. Pablo Picasso might have concurred with him. Picasso once told me, "All painters make bad pictures but only great painters made good ones, once in a while."

Is the masterpiece more archetypal, more masterful, more intense, unique? Is the masterpiece more expressive and stronger? Is it that the masterpiece coincides with similar discoveries in other fields, like the Picasso painting *Les Demoiselles d'Avignon* (1907), which coincided with the work of Emil Durkheim and Lucien Levy-Bruhl and the beginning of anthropology and ethnography?

I think it is more precise to say that the "masterpiece" can be singled out of a continuum that is constituted by the general unfolding of the artist's creativity. More than a purely subjective catharsis, can a masterpiece be considered as *a new emblem where a whole generation and more can recognize an image of what was heretofore unconscious for all?* I feel that Oremland's view easily accommodates to this way of considering the masterpiece.

The power of a new concept or of a masterpiece is that even if it goes unrecognized or triggers opposition, it divides time between a before and an after. After Galileo the Earth became round for the Church, which condemned him, as well as for those of his contemporaries who could not read or write. It became a "fact" pregnant with consequences valid for all.

It seems to me that the notion of a "new emblem" is a useful concept when considered in relation to women's creativity. Simone de Beauvoir (1949) spoke well to a gender difference in *Le Deuxième Sexe*. De Beauvoir offered that women are more interested in integration and totality than in rejecting norms or indulging in exercises of style. In my words, they prefer the Cosmic egg and its contents to the actual breaking of it.

A medium in which women have always excelled is literature. Starting in ancient Greece with the poet Sappho, who expressed a kind of love not given to men, to Christine de Pisan who in the fourteenth century wrote *La Cité des Dames*. De Pisan, a champion of women, dedicated her last poem in 1429 to the defense of Joan of Arc. In the sixteenth century, Marguerite de Navarre, sister of Francis I of France, not only protected the poet Clement Marot, accused of sympathy for the Huguenots' heretic creed, but wrote mystical hymns touched by the reformation spirit. The same princess was also the famous author of the *Heptameron*, a book of tales full of irony and wit. Also, during the sixteenth century, a bourgeois woman from Lyon, the poet Louise Labé, nicknamed "La belle Cordière," became and remained to this day known for her sonnets and for *The Debate Between Madness and Love*. In the seventeenth century Marie-Madeleine de La Fayette published anonymously three novels, one of which, *La Princesse de Clèves* (1678), is considered a masterpiece and one of the high points of classic literature. The interest in *La Princesse de Clèves* does not depend on the plot or its incidents but on the fine analysis of characters, the crystalline clarity of thought, and the perfection of its prose. She was a friend of the Marquise de Sevigné, author of famous *Letters*.

Toward the end of the eighteenth century, between October 1796 and August 1797, Jane Austen wrote her first novel, *Pride and Prejudice*. The classic was not published until 1813 because of the publishers' lack of enthusiasm. During the nineteenth century many women adopted masculine pennames in order to avoid opposition from publishers and public alike; George Sand and George Elliot are examples. Apart from her novels, George Sand's best works could be her abundant correspondence, especially with Gustave Flaubert. On the other side of the Channel, George Elliot produced undisputed masterpieces—*Silas Marner, The Mill on the Floss,* and *Middlemarch. Wuthering Heights* by Emily Brontë is both powerful and original, revealing a seldom equaled intensity of feeling.

With the twentieth century, women's contributions to culture remained as remarkable and became more frequent. Just listing Edith Wharton, Colette, Virginia Woolf, Gertrude Stein, and more recently Marguerite Yourcenar and Simone de Beauvoir, to name only a few, gives an idea of the importance of their achievements. All of these women gave voice to the silent half of humanity. They did not duplicate male artists' depictions of both sexes and the world. They unveiled other viewpoints, perspectives, and motivations. In France, Colette was the first woman to be elected to the prestigious Academie Goncourt, one of ten members, and Marguerite Yourcenar was the first woman to be elected to be one of the forty members of the French Academy, an institution founded in the fifteenth century by Cardinal Richelieu.

Another field where women have displayed absolute originality is the field of choreography. There are many, but mentioning Isadora Duncan, Doris Humphrey, and Martha Graham is enough. They broke through formalized routines, liberated the dancer from academic constraints, and invented a natural language of the body that allowed for forceful expression of human passions.

In the visual arts, at first women's only access to the tools and the training was within the family. Women were not allowed to study from nude models or belong to the guilds. An exception was the making of stained glass windows, a birthright privilege of the nobility. Among the artists whose names and works have come to us, Artemisia Gentileschi (1593–1653), Louise Moillon (1609–1696), Angelica Kauffman (1741–1807), Elizabeth Vigée-Lebrun (1755–1842), and Rosa Bonheur (1822–1899), all had in common that their fathers were painters. Some others like Sofonisba Anguissola (1532–1625) were scions of aristocratic families. By the latter part of the nineteenth century with the ascendancy of the bourgeoisie, some women whose families allowed the development of their vocation or who had other financial means to support themselves began to appear as artists. At the turn of the century, along with the other Impressionists, young women such as Berthe Morisot, Mary Cassatt, and Eva Gonzalez could bloom.

A great change came with Suzanne Valadon. Valadon, who was from the working class, started life as an acrobat, and became a model after a fall from the trapeze. Thanks to the encouragement of Edgar Degas, who admired her drawings, Valadon became a strongly motivated, individualistic artist, one very well known in the first half of the twentieth century. As Oremland rightly points out, "The patron is the unsung hero in creativity."

Valadon is testimony to the fact that by the turn of the century, if a women had the will, even if she did not have the means, and if she were prepared to face as much hardship if not more than her male colleagues, she could paint. With the onset of the twentieth century, the list becomes long: Gwen John, Romaine Brooks, Cecilia Beaux, Natacha Goncharova, Lliuba Popova, Rosanova, Gabrielle Munter, Paula Modersohn-Becker,

Kathe Köllwitz, Georgia O'Keeffe, Vanessa Bell, Marie Laurencin, Sonia Delaunay, the sculptor Camille Claudel, Tamara de Lempicka, the sculptor Barbara Hepworth, Lee Krasner, Vieira da Silva, Frida Kalho, Louise Bourgeois, Isabel Bishop, Dorothea Tanning, Leonore Fini, not to mention anyone from the more contemporary generations.

In the field of music it seems that until now there have not been great female composers. In architecture we are only beginning to acknowledge women architects.

Because female artists are not as numerous as their male counterparts, does it mean that anatomy is destiny and that creativity is related to gender? I feel that Oremland is accurate in delinking creativity and gender and in proposing that creativity transcends gender.

Yet, as Oremland notes there is the question of children and creativity. The burden of paternity is certainly less than the burden of maternity. The creative genius Jean-Jacques Rousseau elected to abandon his children, an action that very few women could consider.

In addition to internal differences regarding the male and the female's relation to having a child, alluded to by Oremland, the interaction between the artist and society is different according to their gender. Male artists leading a Bohemian existence are often considered eccentric marginals and antisocial rebels and admired for their unconventionality. Women artists behaving the same way cannot count on the indulgence of public opinion. They become unredeemable reprobates. Many gifted women selected not to have romantic adventures and not to procreate since they wanted to create. Yet such self-restraint can lead to a drying up of the wellspring of emotions, particularly later in life. I suggest that a great woman artist need not fear experiencing life to the fullest since the source of creativity is linked to the deepest and most intense of our "pulsions." I fear women are more sensitive to exclusion than men and that the fear of being an outcast may have been a great deterrent in the past. I feel that fear is less today.

Nowadays in Western countries women can enter most professions, answer any inner calling without more impediment than having to face their own fears, inhibitions, and anxieties. Whether married or single they can continue to work when they have children and bring them up without necessarily being branded "bad mothers." Enlightened love rather than quantity of love is being given its just due.

Another valuable point raised by Oremland in relation to creativity is the importance he gives to *the patron*. The patron can be nurturing or, as Oremland noted, like a parent, an obstacle to the artist. I have noted that patrons, male and female alike, have a tendency to be more interested in male than in female artists. I wonder if Oremland's idea of the patron as a "reincarnation" of the transitional mother helps explain this bias—another subtle representation of the preference for the male child. As noted by Oremland, the patron can be a teacher, a critic, or an institution, such as a university or a museum. In fact in the twentieth century, for the visual arts, the patron is most often the art dealer.

Some art galleries actually have quotas—implicit and explicit agreements that no more than one or two female artists to a dozen or more males will be under contract and shown. In general less support and certainly less publicity is given to the careers of female artists than male artists, unless the female artists are only decorative or repetitive artists and less dangerous competitors. It is only during the last fifteen years that women artists demanding to be taken seriously are treated accordingly.

Many factors are currently changing, giving new hope and opportunity for women's creativity, including the fact that women are becoming independent financially. Recently enough professional women have become sufficiently affluent to afford to collect works by women. I see this interest as more than social shifts and changing recognition. *I feel that more women are becoming interested in the art of women because they find women's creations more meaningful to them—that women artists speak to "the hidden side of the moon."*

To conclude, *The Origins and Psychodynamics of Creativity* is a provocative text with an original, positive attitude toward creativity. The book strikes me as being reflective of and congenial to the thinking and the affect of imaginative people. The book will help creative people see more clearly where problems are and where solutions might be. I was pleased to be asked by Dr. Oremland for my spontaneous reactions to his manuscript. My responses may or may not be quite congruent with what he means. For that I hope he will absolve me.

A Director Responds

Carey Perloff

In this study, Jerome Oremland theorizes that creativity is related to the development of an integrated, differentiated sense of self and other. This struck a resonant chord with my musings on the nature of creativity as it relates to my work as a stage director and as a teacher of actors.

In some deep way I have always experienced creativity as an indefinable sense of longing. In the middle of rehearsals for Anton Chekhov's *Uncle Vanya* at the American Conservatory Theater in San Francisco, as we wrestled with the nature of ordinary characters with extraordinary passions and desires, it occurred to me that creativity is particularly powerful because it is a desire that is never satiated, a desire that continually cries out to be exercised. This subjective sense seems close to Oremland's idea that a cardinal characteristic of creativity is that it begins early and continues throughout life. I feel sure that any creative individual feels this sense of urgency and the extraordinary pleasure in experiencing the creative act. I also feel that creativity, if not regularly activated, atrophies. I find that my

---

Ms. Perloff is the Artistic Director of the American Conservatory Theater, San Francisco, California.

most creative times are times when I have just come off another project.

Unlike a painter or poet who can return to the solitude of the studio to create, a performing artist becomes a part of the entire creative event for work to be formed. Perhaps this is why I always become restless when I have been out of the rehearsal process for too long. As interesting and engaging as other aspects of my life as an artistic director may be, nothing even approximates the sensation of life being fully lived in the moment like rehearsal. I may be describing something close to what Oremland calls "my first love." I look upon the rehearsal process not as a series of tasks leading to a finished product, but as a connected series of creative events, each with its own integrity and its own forward velocity. Even in the early stages of rehearsal, entire playlets can emerge and subside in the space of moments, each with its own coherence and integrity.

I find the difference between creative directors and "hack" directors (I would include actors) is the difference in the way they use the rehearsal process. For a creative director (and actors), the rehearsal is a free-form exploration within definite boundaries in which a journey can and does occur. This seems close to Oremland's relating creativity to play. For a "hack" artist the rehearsal is a job, an execution of already formulated ideas, a dead recitation of a previously conceived plan. This is not the same as Oremland's idea regarding the role of propagandizing in the production of hackneyed work. I have in mind something rote, contrived, and repetitious with too heavy an eye on the result than on the creation.

The great British director Peter Brook (1987) explores these differences regarding directing in his seminal book *The Empty Space*. Brook describes his development from the days he regarded the director as a mover of live chess pieces to his current view of the director as the trigger of the collective imagination of the group of collaborators. A thrilling rehearsal, as Brook eloquently revealed, is always a venture into the unknown, and the great challenge is to have the courage to go wherever the journey might lead, within the construct of the particular world view being explored. This sense of new exploration and new symbol formation is what Oremland describes as "transitional functioning."

Because the directing journey is always interactive and the energy for the journey comes from the collision of artists in the room, the rehearsal event is both deeply personal and completely transpersonal. The creativity I feel as a director in rehearsal is rarely "self-generated" but is generated by my own free interaction with the text, what Oremland describes as "internal dialogue" with the author. This dialogue between the author and me interacts with the visual world of the play, the actors, the music, and the space around me. For me, and I am sure this is true of most creative individuals, it is critical that I work on a play that stimulates and inspires me, and that I am collaborating with artists who can both produce and receive a wide variety of ideas and stimuli. Short of that, the event has nothing to do with art and everything to do with making "product."

In a creative rehearsal, ideas are traded quickly and freely, they metamorphose and evolve, are shaped and discarded. "Happy accidents" litter the rehearsal room. For example, I was recently working on the elliptical David Storey play *Home*, a play about four people in a mental home. In the middle of the long opening *pas de deux* between the two men, one of the actors realized that he had left his glove on the other side of the table. Rather than interrupting the rehearsal to ask me when I would like him to retrieve it, he engineered a brilliant subterfuge whereby the glove was stolen back without the other character seeing it happen. This "glove lazzi" became clearly useful in delineating the kind of paranoia that lurked beneath the meticulously polite British behavior of these characters. Since *Home* revolves around its characters' desperate dislocation from their own histories and from their own "possessions" (one is never quite sure what belongs to whom), the chance discovery of the glove game became a fruitful and interesting epitomizing point.

The director's job is to mold the combined creative energies into a coherent final product. Inevitably, however, the rehearsal process comes to an end. The product may be beautiful and of great satisfaction, but the exhilarating moment-to-moment life of the rehearsal process is over. The actors must be released to continue the process themselves with an audience, and without a director. The end is a period of mourning for a director. I would add this experience to Oremland's many analogies between the creator and the created object and parent and child.

Very little that I have ever read about creativity explains the creative process and the way the mind works creatively. Oremland's work is an exciting exception. Much of the creativity of directing is in collaboration with designers, actors, composers, choreographers, set designers, and many others. The most creative sessions I have had with any group of collaborating artists on a play involve a kind of *intuitive* problem solving in which the mind leaps from step to step in a sort of free-associative dream logic—a sort of mental improvisation in which, as Oremland describes, the conscious–unconscious dichotomy disappears. At the same time, the boundaries (budget, size, and shape of the theater space itself and the nature of the material) in the kind of creativity that I am involved with are clear. Within these boundaries, anything can happen in the same way that, as Oremland points out, within the confines of a commission, a painter conjures what he or she will.

Very often, as one talks through a problem in a play one realizes that one is referencing stored information or images of which one was not aware, or that a solution has suddenly emerged "whole" from one's mind without any prior knowledge—an epiphany. I am astonished at how much of our mental life goes on without our awareness; Oremland well describes how much is packed, condensed he calls it, into a creative idea. A great deal of the creative process has to do with sensing how far one can take a given idea, how "fertile" that idea is, and how to know when it has yielded all that it will yield.

A current example from the design phase of a complex production of Euripides' *Hecuba*: One of the great problems to be solved with any Greek tragedy is the question of the Chorus. How does one handle the idea of collective thought and collective speech in a world in which such things are utterly foreign without making them seem "foreign" on stage? I had been reading recently about refugees, since the world once again seems to be filled with huge populations of displaced people, from Ruwanda to Bosnia to Kobe, Japan, desperately trying to reconnect themselves to some semblance of normalcy. *Hecuba* is a play about a group of displaced women, Trojan women, whom the Greek army has captured through duplicity (the famous Trojan Horse episode). As the play opens, these women and the entire Greek army are moored on the ragged coast of Thrace, awaiting favorable winds to return them to Greece. The first part of the play represents a dream Hecuba has been having for three nights about her only remaining son Polydorus, whom she fears has been killed. The Chorus appears to tell Hecuba that the Greeks have decided to sacrifice her daughter as an offering to Achilles to cause the winds to change.

The emotional tenor of this particular Chorus cries out to be sung. About a year before, I walked into a church in Berkeley and heard the explosive, mysterious nasal music of a group called Kitka. I knew immediately that they were going to be my Greek Chorus. I hired a composer, David Lang, with whom I frequently collaborate. He began creating a particular, haunting sound for this group of women vis-à-vis *Hecuba*. Lang's sound evolved for about a year. In a design session, the set and lighting designers, the choreographer, and I met to talk about the "tents" these women were to live in (according to Euripides). Ostensibly we were meeting to solve a particular technical problem about how these tents could be constructed given that they had to be torn down each night at the end of the play.

Creative breakthroughs frequently seem to emerge from the analysis of a mundane problem. This time was no exception. As we talked, a series of questions swirled around in the back of my mind. What was the stage life of these women, the Kitka singers, going to involve? How was I going to imbue a group of nonactors with the imaginative life necessary to fill their performances on stage? How could we personalize the tents to such a degree that when at the end of the play they are torn down by the Thracian ruler, the audience experiences a true violation? As we were talking, an idea occurred to me seemingly out of nowhere but utterly complete. The action of the Chorus in this play would be to build their structures themselves in live time during the course of the play. Whatever "scenery" the audience saw would evolve from the women themselves. The women would gather whatever materials they could scrounge from the barren landscape around them, decorating them with personal adornments, perhaps with articles of their own clothing, to lure the Thracian king Polymestor into a beautiful trap that he would destroy. Thus the visual world would evolve in complexity and emotion exactly as the play itself does. The women would be woven into the central fabric of the play's action, not as witnesses but as creators of the life being lived.

Weeks later came an important workshop in which we tested the efficacy of this idea. We led Kitka into a room filled with flotsam and jetsam: wet nets, pieces of wood, long strips of cloth, shells, some jewelry, etc. We asked them to create shelter for themselves out of what they found. For an hour and a half, we sat and watched, captivated, as a whole life began to be lived in the room. Long rows of women on their knees began wringing out wet netting and passing it down the line to be placed in piles. Big arcs of cloth were thrown into the air to catch onto wooden planks wedged into benches to provide support. Bits of raffia were carefully woven into the cloth and nets to create an entire tissue covering the wooden frame. Finally flowers, jewels, and bits of personal clothing were artfully arranged around the "doorway," along the crest of the structure, and bordering the floor. When it felt complete, the women went inside the "tent," closed the door flap, and slowly began to sing a lament.

Through a simple task, these nonactors had found a deeply personal connection to a real life experience, without any verbal communication among each other or coaching from us. It was an incredible moment. Rather than a series of tents, which is what I expected, they created a single structure that encompassed them because that is where the need was most deeply felt. Nothing that they did looked like "acting" or like those awful artificial moments on stage in which life stops and bad imitation begins. It seemed simple; as if the idea had always been there just waiting to be articulated and tested.

In any art form, one can mystify the process, but in the final analysis it comes down to some intuitive sense. Perhaps this is why creative people are deeply pragmatic, and why there is a sense of clarity, however arcane, about a creative solution. Creative people seem to have a powerful sense of what works and what does not in the moment, in real time, not theoretically but actually, in the instant. This echoes Oremland's idea about parsimony and absence of redundancy and ambiguity in creativity. The artists with whom I like to work are "present tense" and attuned.

As example, I was in rehearsal with Harold Pinter for his play *The Birthday Party*, which we were producing almost in the round in an off-Broadway theater in New York. Pinter had only seen his work performed in a proscenium theater. An aspect of our set that especially interested him was that the stage directions called for a staircase off left which is usually hidden by the proscenium. Because our set was a free-floating platform in the middle of the space, the staircase became a dominant motif, a spindly avenue to a no-man's land up above.

Of course it created marvelous entrance and exit opportunities, which Pinter, the consummate actor, appreciated. One day as he was watching rehearsals he could not resist anymore. He leaned over and said to me, "I would like to add a line. When Meg exits, I would like her to say as she disappears up above 'What a lovely flight of stairs'." *The Birthday Party* had been performed dozens of times in its twenty-five-year history, but at that moment, with that set and those actors, Pinter knew it needed that new line. His addition worked brilliantly every night.

Recently I have been engaged in training actors, another fascinating window onto creativity. We all recognize that on some level great acting is un-self-conscious, yet paradoxically it requires enormous consciousness and technique to attain that level of un-self-consciousness. When one watches children at play, there is a level of spontaneous connection and expression that begins to disappear at about age 6. Beyond that point, one must learn *all* over again how to play, how to live in the moment without stopping the impulse or censoring what's actually happening. I believe this is what Oremland means when he differentiates play from games.

Indeed much of actor training is related to the art of playing in the present moment, so that ultimately what an audience is watching is not a codified performance that has already been lived, but life in the making. There are lots of different metaphors for this. One can talk to actors about being part of a "flow," about the sensation of "taking a ride." But when it happens, the part of the mind that wants to plan, predict, and judge is released and another part, a part that is alive, awake, impulsive, and trained to react, takes over. The objective of actor training is twofold: to create supple, flexible, intelligent "instruments" (in terms of voice, physical life, level of literacy, and so on) through which specific kinds of emotions can pass, and then (which is infinitely more difficult) to develop techniques to trigger these emotions via the language of the play into forming encounters that are always surprising and always present tense. There is acting that *describes* experience and acting that *is* experience.

Bertolt Brecht insisted that while a stage need not be littered with extraneous bits of reality, those actions that are performed (whether it is sawing wood or sewing a button) must be absolutely real and not just "indicated." Then the actions will represent life being lived and not life being described. Acting that *is* experience is different every night and depends upon many variables, including the ever-evolving exchange between actors night to night and the fascinating and unpredictable interaction between a live audience and actors. The rhythm and mood and "connectedness" of an audience become part of the current into which the actor must step each night to "play." And "play" it is, serious play, in which the stakes are high but the kaleidoscope is always moving. Oremland approaches these considerations in his discussion of the "unseen" audience of creativity and its relationship for performers with the actual audience.

Many American actors have forgotten the word *play*. They are steeped in a kind of post-Stanislavskian technique (sometimes called The Method) in which emotion is generated through a set of preparation exercises that include "prelife" work (evolving a biography of one's character prior to the events in the play), "substitution" (substituting someone or something that one has had an intense emotional reaction to in the past for the character or situation on stage), "inner monologue" and so on. All of these exercises have their place, but I have come to realize that if self-referential psychology becomes too dominant in an actor's work, the creative impulse is stifled. Creativity is not a technique one can learn but a spark that can be nurtured into flame. Creativity can just as quickly be extinguished. Oremland reveals this beautifully in his case studies.

The need for the creative spark to be continually nurtured is acutely felt, which leads me to another area of inquiry in Oremland's book, the relationship of women (and children) to creativity. Does the creative impulse become dulled or less urgent for creative women once they have children? The thought frightens me. I would hope that children enhance creativity rather than stifle it. Certainly they absorb a huge part of one's thought that was formerly free to play and escape. Children force one to be "on" emotionally all the time. However, like any exciting improvisation, children also force one to live moment to moment in the present tense in very palpable ways. Perhaps Oremland and people who have thought about creativity in women underplay how much having children enhances creativity.

Life is acutely experienced by a child, because everything is new. Joy is absolute, as is despair; there are very few grays in the early childhood experience. This is a powerful phenomenon to be around. I found valuable Oremland's many analogies between the child's explorations and the creative individual's continuing exploration of "life anew."

Because every childhood reaction, every gesture, every sound, exists as if for the first time, having children has sharpened my senses about the oddness of our daily world, the Wittgensteinian absurdity of the way we acquire language, the impossibility of balancing on two feet, and the beauty and terror of sleep. A significant part of the creative act lies in defamiliarization, in the act of seeing the familiar in new ways, or of rendering the unfamiliar oddly familiar. That is the daily activity of childhood, and that is probably one of the reasons why the experience of watching my children grow up has been fascinating to me and stimulating to my own work.

I found much familiar, much novel, and much stimulating in Oremland's understanding of creativity. Everything could not be commented upon, but I tried to respond creatively to his ideas by illustrating my responses from my experience in bringing plays to life.

A Sculptor Responds

Aris Demetrios

I am a sculptor, the son of a sculptor, and the father of a sculptor. Essentially, I went into the family business, sculpting. I now observe that I have done things more like a journeyman image maker of the medieval guilds than the modern artist going into the world full of hope in the 1960s in California. In Oremland's

---

Aris Demetrios, an acclaimed sculptor, is the winner of two national competitions, the White Memorial Fountain, Stanford University, and the Corregidor/Bataan National Monument.

distinguishing talent from creativity, I see much that reflects my experience as I traveled from the reactive to the creative state of mind.

I began my professional career thirty years ago by entering competitions to do large sculptures in large public spaces. No doubt ambition and competition with my father were among the driving forces. The size of works ranged from eight to eighty feet. I was fortunate not to be bound by traditional methods for proceeding from the maquette state to the large finished work. What bothered me was that most big stuff looked lifeless when finally installed. To me it was the difference between the imperiousness of the gigantic statues of Imperial Rome and the quiet humanity of Roman portraiture. Learning to preserve the vitality of the piece as it got bigger became my task.

I studied architecture, but the reductive methods of design did not produce an answer. After trial and error, I realized that the artistic task was not making the perfect sculpture but learning how to anticipate and approximate the finished work in scale and size before it was done.

In sculpture anticipation is difficult because one has to fight "the armature war." Because of the inherent mass, bulk, and weight of three-dimensional material, one has to support (armature) the material as one is trying to alter it. What was most difficult to ascertain was whether or not the dynamic of the piece would transfer as the size increased. The scale at which each piece arrives demands a different set of form constraints. I believe Oremland writes well about the artist's struggle to maintain a concept as new parameters are encountered.

What became clear was that the work must be continually in process and never leave the domain of one's control, even though every world through which the sculpture passes—the worlds of permits, officialdom, and architecture—conspires against the artist's concept and insists that the artistic process was complete at the end of the design state.

Moreover, the traditional methods of enlarging sculpture were perfected only in the foundries and the carving works where scores of artisans do the work. All of this distances the sculptor from observing and learning from his or her work. I taught myself to weld so that the entire enlarging and fabricating of my work would be in my shop where I could see all of it and learn from the disasters and the triumphs.

One must learn how to extend the doing and undoing, trying and failing, and learning and unlearning that characterize creativity throughout the making of the piece. The artist must come to understand that there are many different competing value systems in the development of art, each with its valid justifications. This is particularly apparent in public art.

I came to realize that to make sculpture larger than the studio, one has to extend the creative process beyond the studio. For example, in the fabrication and installation of the 80-foot red-painted *Cosmos* (1990) (Figure 16), I wanted to orient the sculpture so that the piece would evolve from the simple to the complex as the viewer first saw it on foot or by automobile from the nearby freeway. *Cosmos* consists of three eighty-foot vertical masts holding a configuration of curvilinear shapes at various heights. I aligned the masts such that only two were visible at the entry vista to ensure that elements would unfold themselves as the viewer moves around and even walks under the towering piece.

Achieving this result amounted to a considerable task in that each form weighed tons and, I was told, could only be attached to one reinforced point on the masts. By strengthening the masts and adding innumerable reinforcing points, each element could be moved up or down and be rotated. I was then able to direct the crane by radio from the vista openings a mile away aligning the sculpture on multiple axes. Now *Cosmos* has a sense of life and vitality from the time one first sees it to anywhere on one's approach to and through it. I believe Oremland's concept of condensation is applicable. It was critical that there be many different *Cosmos* in *Cosmos*.

A large sculpture must come to terms with a physical context and often with a political one as well. Unlike the example of

FIGURE 16.   *Cosmos*, Aris Demetrios (1990) (Sculpture Park,
Roseville, California). (Courtesy of Aris Demetrios.)

the Serra sculpture cited by Oremland, the community in which *Cosmos* was to reside was at first more bewildered than antagonistic. The problem became one of trying to encourage the community toward a sense that the art rightfully belonged to them and represented an ongoing experience in which they could participate. To support that goal, the land developer was persuaded to see the sculpture in its next larger frame of reference. He was encouraged to give the local community a substantial endowment, the interest from which supports an ongoing sculpture program in the third and fourth grades in which some two-hundred-fifty children a year study the local flora and fauna with guidance. The children make bas-reliefs. Some ten of these are cast into bronze and installed in an art park surrounding *Cosmos*. At an annual ceremony, I welcome the contributions of my "fellow artists." The subtext of this ceremony underscores the fact that children and the out-of-town artist have shared the making of art. *Cosmos* is now welcome.

I have tried to show how some of the arenas around my sculptures had to be explored and included in the process in order that the work be made and survive. I should like to turn to the making of sculpture and indicate the way in which for me talent became art.

Sculpture, like all art, possesses within itself the possibility to lead the doer from talent to creativity if one listens to, honors, and owns the process of making stuff. This redemptive quality is powerful and present in the everyday doing of the work. One notices the day when the work, which heretofore had been devouring, returns the effort. The work smiles and gives that power back again to the artist. I believe these feelings are close to what Oremland means when he says the art piece is an *object* in the psychoanalytic sense and art making is a kind of *object* relating. Oremland accurately describes the dialogue between the maker and the piece.

I believe talent becomes creativity when such an emotive dialogue exists continually in the studio with the usual and the unusual. One finds oneself composing an ongoing ritual that continually contributes to the ongoing work. Yet in one's workplace, one is also a predator, quick to examine the result of accident, chance, or the deliberative move. Oremland is correct, creating is a relationship and an uneasy one.

Certainly one begins to develop work procedures that reinforce one's particular proclivity. For example, the area around the band saw is not swept and is always cluttered with yesterday's and past remnants and discards. As I clear the saw table to begin the day, I touch and thereby automatically invest myself with a recitative of past concerns. One learns that the creative energies are cyclic; sometimes great outbursts of work are followed by a desert. Creative surges must be embraced; whenever they are there, one must strike.

Sculpture is a marvelous profession. Sculpture lets, or better, requires its maker to use every bit of psyche, soul, mind, hands, heart, and guts to make the work. It is at once visceral and spiritual, each invested in the other. August Strindberg's play *The Creditors* (1888) defines this creative pantheon vividly in the three principals. Adolph, the sculptor, is divided between his animus, Gustav, and his anima, Tekla, his wife. Tekla, intuitive and emotional, learns reason from her former lover, Gustav. Gustav, the didactic critic and destroyer, becomes passionate. Creation becomes destruction. Reason becomes passion. Love becomes hate. Hate becomes love. The artist, Adolph, is consumed by this dueling of opposites and dies. The action takes place in a single day. Metaphorically, in any artist's studio, this is every day playing itself out.

The doing and completing of a sculpture brings with it continuing and marvelous revelations with new possibilities. Should I try this or that? Should it be wood or metal, larger or smaller, above or below, an arc or straight, like or unlike? Should I repeat or not? Each choice becomes a challenge. What does the change do? After one makes the work, the work transforms and it and artist are irrevocably changed. One cannot unlearn the piece.

The possibilities and the perils are great. Any piece can lead to informed intuition or a logjam.

Although my first fifteen years as a sculptor were spent making major sculptures in public spaces, I became aware of a sense of increasing disquiet. Although successful, I was still the journeyman. Even though I did prize-winning fountains, an important clock tower, and various acclaimed kinetic pieces, there was a growing sense of dissatisfaction. After some introspection, I concluded that I had lost my direction and inner sense of continuity.

With the cooperation of wife and family, I stopped the commissioned work to begin to study sculpture again from a new perspective. Although the primary assumption was that I knew nothing, of course there was always something consistent about the things that I liked. For over two years, I traveled to each piece of modern sculpture that I admired. I drew it to understand it. Until I read it in Oremland, I did not know that this was the same method that Freud (1914) used to understand the *Moses*. Sometimes I made a three-dimensional maquette. Tentatively, I began to make maquettes, which at first looked like Moores, Martinis, and Smiths. Gradually a signature of my own emerged. I knew I had found my voice when I learned to draw in blocks of wood with a band saw.

Better still, I found, and now own, that deep inner flow that seems to proceed from the center. Sometimes this current is so strong that I feel that I am the singer not the song composer and that the songs I sing come from somewhere else. Sometimes the urge to create is so compelling that every step in the making of a series of pieces has an inevitability about it. Oremland's writing on the passage from inspiration to manifestation rings true. He describes well how the progression is filled with epiphany, ecstasy, and intense disappointments.

Considering the progressions in creativity brings me to an absolute, the trust of the intuitive, a trust that did not come easily given my heritage and education. I find that if in composing in the beginning I try to name, title, label, or verbally question anything, the flow of the piece diminishes or subsides altogether. However, once the maquette exists outside of me, I challenge, criticize, and often toss it away. What is amazing is how much logic and rigor comes from the intuitive side. If I were to dream about today's piece tonight, all the dialogue, intuitive and critical, would be there.

Oremland speaks rightly about creativity and the sense of play. Creativity is play that is only at times fun. Precisely because creativity is play, because the inhibitions and prohibitions are gone, one can alter, move, cantilever, omit, smash, and cherish any part of anything that comes. An informing illustration was Robert Rauschenberg's slinging an automobile tire around the waist of a stuffed goat that stood astride a painting and observing "Why not?"

All sculptors will say that they create, but not all sculptors can create a paradigm change. However, if one has come to trust one's way of making an honest piece, the piece may turn out good or even great. The surest way not to make a masterpiece is to set out to do just that.

Recently I have been working in several directions, one of which developed from observing that when I cut in steel plate a figure from its ground, the drop (negative space) was as intriguing an entity as the positive. I began separating one from the other. This led me to think about using pairs in a work. I could use pairs of things that were alike and not alike. Certainly my readings in Western literature led me to observe how often in the West human conditions are described in polarities—good and evil, free will and destiny, male and female, and creation and destruction. I appreciate Oremland's emphasis on symmetry as the fundament of art but believe it should be extended to the dualities.

At the beginning of my Portal Series, in *Portal Series I* (1992) (Figure 17), I placed the image of a woman, arms proudly held high, flipped atop the rectangular plate from which the shape had been cut. The synergy of the piece suggests an act completing, the one complementing and fulfilling the other. Carrying the

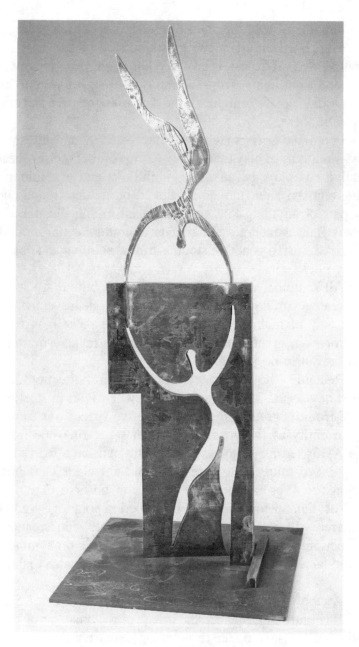

FIGURE 17. *Portal Series I*, Aris Demetrios (1992) (Private
Collection, Pebble Beach, California). (Courtesy of Aris Demetrios.)

notion further, in *My Space* (1992) (Figure 18), four figures are aloft, hand to hand, juggled by the lower figure who steps through the negative space of the drop. *My Space* is the wonderful space of creativity—joyous, profound, hopeful, and full of possibility. Perhaps this makes visible what Oremland calls the *location* of creativity.

Perhaps the notion of the *holon*, a word coined by Arthur Koestler from the Greek for whole, is apt here. By twisting, hinging, manipulating, changing, omitting, and altering the scale of the elements and coupling these with strategies of fragmentation and repetition, one develops a rich palette of forms and ideas with which one can begin to deal with universals.

Much of my material comes from my dream world. I was struck by Oremland's statement that art is an externalized dream. I find that after many years of honoring my dreams, I have learned to be active in them, to take part in them, and to shape them. I dream often of composing, playing with, and understanding sculpture. In a dream, it is fascinating to walk around *inside* a mass and feel the forces in it. Like many, I have found that a problem whose solution has eluded me will suddenly present itself complete in a dream or in the trancelike state that I seem to enter when I meander in my studio at the end of the day. I liked Oremland's insistence that the conscious–unconscious polarity disappears in creativity.

I have also begun a series of pieces trying to develop a narrative vocabulary. As I continue, I find that in a strange way, by positing some passages as dualities, I can choreograph a much denser set of images. The images are those of the world around us, full of contradictory forces, ambivalences, hopes, and confusion. One is an image from a Wendell Berry poem about a man running on a flimsy scaffolding, *Scaffolding Series I* (1992), (Figure 19), on which if he ran fast enough, the structure will not collapse. As I worked on the piece, I found that I had to build a rickety construct, not a firm safe structure, in order for the piece to evolve.

FIGURE 18. *My Space*, Aris Demetrios (1992) (Private Collection, Gainesville, Florida). (Courtesy of Aris Demetrios.)

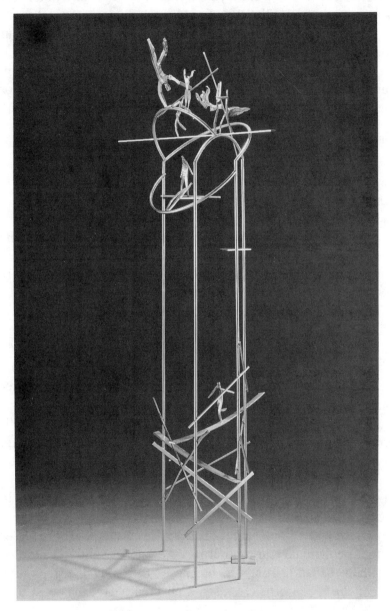

FIGURE 19. *Scaffolding Series I*, Aris Demetrios (1992) (Private Collection, Petaluma, California). (Courtesy of Aris Demetrios.)

At present, I am uneasy. The disquiet is back. I think that there is another domain that I should reach. I know it is inaccessible solely by reason. It may be awakened in a dream or occur spontaneously. It may be concealed by my skills. Is this talent as a defense against creativity that Oremland describes? To begin again, so to speak, I am starting to draw with a stick instead of a pen and using my other hand. I look forward to what may come.

A Businessman Responds

Thomas Perkins

In responding to Jerome Oremland's request to participate in his book on creativity and before reading the manuscript, I proffered the observation that creativity cannot be learned but that probably it can be understood. He readily agreed.

But is this not an apparent paradox? Even though many, perhaps most, of one's various skills and abilities come through education, understanding, training, and practice, creativity seems to be something quite apart. Oremland quite usefully draws the distinction between talent that can indeed be developed and creativity that can be nurtured but not engendered.

Creativity seems to derive from powerful, unconscious wellsprings a priori. Oremland sees an analogy among dreaming, playing, and creating. As clearly a dream cannot be created by partners or a committee, so the creative process is highly individual. Talent on the other hand is found and often developed in groups.

Oremland's book largely focuses on visual and to a lesser degree, performance art and artists. Perhaps a valid question is: Can there be an "artist" in business? Certainly the pejorative idea of the "con artist" exists. Can creativity truly exist at a

---

A venture capital investor, Thomas Perkins is a founding partner of Kleiner, Perkins, Caufield, & Byers.

level comparable to the arts in commercial fields where standardization of procedures (business law, accounting, and so forth) are necessarily intrinsic? I know it can occur. In my own career sometimes I think it has actually happened.

My field is high technology venture capital, and while a number of the enterprises I have launched have become famous, I think my creativity, if it exists at all, is not in the choice or organization of these companies (this may be a talent) but rather in setting in place new forms of enabling financial structure and in the direction of the developing organization. Detailing much of this is beyond the scope of these thoughts but I will give examples of structure and of direction so that the reader will have a better notion of what I have in mind.

One of my ventures was the first biotechnology (genetic engineering) company. It was organized to exploit the emerging science and particularly to develop new pharmaceuticals. The financial problem was how does one raise sufficient capital to fund the years of extremely expensive development to support clinical trials required for Food and Drug Administration approval only after which meaningful revenue would be achieved. One solution I created was literally to package these losses and sell them to investors in the form of newly formed Research and Development Limited Partnerships. This new structure converted expenses to revenue enabling the fledgling company to achieve early profitability. The structure required a "rethinking," indeed a playing with, the numerous rules governing tax (and other) accounting and various Securities and Exchange Commission requirements.

By rethinking I mean reexamining the fundamental nature of the profit and loss statement of an enterprise. This column is headed by revenue from which are subtracted expenses resulting in either a profit or a loss at the bottom line. But for the new venture there would be no initial product sales, hence no revenue. All the expenses would be reported as loss. But what if the expenses could be somehow converted into revenue? By "playing" with this idea (musing about it, revisiting it, toying with the assumptions) I realized that if the expenses could be under-written by an arms-length third party then this new entity, the partnership, could "hire" the company to perform the research. The funding would thus enter the profit and loss statement as revenue and cancel all the ensuing expenses. The new venture could thus "break even" from the beginning. This new financial package also included tax benefits and capital gain possibilities for the investors. At first it seemed radical, shocking, and to stand conventional accounting on its head. The structure withstood all assaults and was subsequently widely copied with hundreds of millions of dollars raised. It enabled the new industry to gain a foothold, which perhaps otherwise might not have occurred.

Earlier, I had perfected a patentable invention in laser optics that proved to be reasonably important and there may have been a similarity in approach. The problem was that early (continuous gas) lasers were unstable because the interferometer mirrors were too vibration and temperature sensitive. Great efforts were ap-plied to reduce the problem, for example, by mounting the plasma tube and mirrors on granite making the device cumber-some and expensive. My rethinking of the problem led to the solution of putting the mirrors inside the tube. This was new and permitted the device to become both inexpensive and ultrareli-able. Like a light bulb, the new laser would work in difficult environments, even underwater, and a host of new applications flowed from the invention.

In both examples, the key idea was to restructure essentially everything. Expenses became revenue, the laser was turned in-side out, or more accurately, outside in. Both solutions were really quite simple, but their "newness" was unique.

While Oremland might disagree, for me it is too great a stretch to relate a "masterpiece" in business to anything in the visual arts by any plastic arts master, be it painter or sculptor. But, perhaps it is a lesser stretch to compare the creative busi-nessman to a creative film director or a creative film producer. I think they have very much in common, particularly as the film or business develops past its initial concept.

Both must have a clear view, the idea, of the overall result desired. But both must necessarily work with a variety of other people to see the conception to its ultimate fulfillment. Along the way the others, be they actors or engineers, will interact with the idea and divert or modify it. The director, either film or business, must on something of an ad hoc, spur of the moment basis, change, build, and modify. If he is creative his original conception may be retained or even enhanced; if not, failure or the banal may result.

An example from my experience may illustrate this directing process. A company was formed to develop a new technology to create an improved ultrasound medical imaging device. The technology promised the possibility of imaging resolution roughly five times greater than competitive devices. The engineers indeed delivered this result, unfortunately at a manufacturing cost of twice that planned, leading to a sales price more than double that of the most expensive product on the market, a product of limited penetration because of its price.

This could have been an unsuccessful situation. As the key director (Chairman of the Board), I was able to restate the equation and playing with the underlying premises, I introduced the new product as the first entry into an entirely new field: the new era and science of "computed sonography." Thus the product did not need to be priced against competition for there was no competition. Because of the underlying merit of the technology, this idea was seized by management and it caught hold. The company is now listed on the New York Stock Exchange.

The creative film director, I believe, is continuously required to play, that is, use, redefine, and interpret within the confines of budget and script. Ad hoc innovations are frequent. The best, as Lawrence Olivier demonstrated in his film masterpiece *Richard III,* creates thrilling new interpretations. The innovative scene in which Richard slides down a bell rope to command the kneeling respect of his startled nobles is unforgettable and was apparently introduced by Olivier (the director) at the last moment. In a single master stroke, layers of understanding of Richard's true character are revealed.

I suspect that people skills, that is to say the people-oriented talent of the director and the business leader are similar. Unlike other creative endeavors, both carry a responsibility to "make it happen." If the nature of their creativity is related, then we may be able to identify some common characteristics between them and with other artists as well. I offer the following areas as promising places to look: motivation, scope, detachment, assurance, and the role of the patron. I will again (immodestly) refer to my own history and personality in the following discussion.

The salient characteristic of the creative is that they create, they produce. Of course, for masters whose individual and specific works may be of equal excellence, there is a vast difference in the volume of output; compare, for example, the total opus of J. S. Bach and Erik Satie. Notwithstanding variation in the intensity of motivation, one does not decide to be creative, one is compelled to try. Whether one is successful or merely another tiresome hack depends on factors well beyond the charter of these thoughts to analyze.

I am aware that in my case the motivation has been very strong and indeed obvious to others. I have been told more than once that I radiate tension. I believe that this drive originated in childhood (I am an only child) and was engendered by the interaction of my parents during the depression era of the 1930s. My mother craved security and fine things that my father could not provide. I believe that I came to feel that the route to her affection was through achievement and success. But of course, it was impossible for the child to play the father's role and further, the harder I tried and as results were obtained, the more I earned the enmity of my father, who resented and denigrated achievement by anyone as a threat. One can see how an impossible cycle developed given these dynamics; a child is striving for mother's love and father's respect, neither of which were obtainable through the striving. The psychological dynamic remains in place. My supposition is that every creative individual has such a wellspring of motivation that is the salient and dominating characteristic in his creative life.

Redefining boundaries, that is, playing with scope is a characteristic of creativity. *Play* is, I think, the proper word and I think Oremland makes a useful distinction between *play* and *game*. I see the creative artist as constantly broadening his scope, redefining the boundaries, reexamining the rules, and sometimes reinventing the game. In business one frequently hears the phrase "the game plan" and to me it is appropriate. One is fortunate, I believe, as work and play become interchangeable to effect this duality more easily. The business world, at least in high technology, is very complex. The rules span a broad spectrum of scientific, legal, regulatory, political, and other parameters. When viewed as a game to be played the very complexity is an opportunity. The solutions exist in the thicket of problems. They can be found and the rules of the game revisited endlessly as situations change and the creative businessman plays with the realities. The game becomes play with endless new vistas.

As I see it, hand in hand with playing with the scope, perhaps paradoxically, is a degree of detachment on the part of the artist. He must *see* the activity as a form of play. He needs a degree of objectivity and self-examination. He needs a detached overview in order to understand that the rules *can* be reinvented, redefined. He must not be so caught up in the game that he misses playing with subtle changes and trends.

Staff meetings, board meetings, presentations, and just about all interactions with others in the business world are opportunities for excitement and fun for me. When viewed as play and with the requisite detachment, even confrontations where the stakes are very high indeed need not be feared or be overly bruising or unduly damaging. Having said all of the above, I cannot pretend that it does not hurt to be tackled, no matter how frequently one reminds oneself that it is only a game.

A curious kind of self-assurance (self-confidence) is also, I believe, a characteristic common among the creative, and I see it as a contributor to and not a result of the creative process. We

are all familiar with the frequently seemingly monumental ego
of the artistic personality, a self-confidence that at times crosses
over the border and becomes indistinguishable from arrogance.
I too, unfortunately, have been accused of making this border
crossing. What looks like lack of self-doubt is essential to creativity. In my case, anyway, I have frequently proceeded without an
apparent understanding of the risks, or so it has seemed to others.
I have been teased about using the phrase "How can I lose?"
when, of course, there were countless ways I could and sometimes did indeed lose. Yet this confidence is not akin to playing
the gambler's "hunch." In fact, I am not at all fond of gambling
and see no parallel in business to its randomness.

In my case at least, the apparent lack of self-doubt springs
from the way the creative idea is formed. The idea is usually
born fully formed and complete. It seems to be "discovered"
rather than developed. It emerges suddenly. It arrives without
qualifications as somehow all of the countervailing forces and
problems have been synthesized into the new idea, the new solution. In this sense, it is perfect. At the time I have utter confidence
in its perfection. Therefore, why should I have doubts, "How
can I lose?" Thus, action can very swiftly follow and usually
does. It would be interesting to explore this feeling of perfection
with creative people in the recognized arts to see if they experience it in the same way.

It is perhaps in this "perfection" that we see the analog
with the dream most clearly. Even dreams that, upon waking,
seem silly or mad, were, while being experienced, logical and
internally consistent. That is what is fascinating and wonderful
about them, how the world of the dream becomes entirely plastic
and is molded to the deeper need for psychological consistency
and "perfection." Similarly, the creative idea seems to mold and
restructure previously perceived reality to a new deeper view and
perfection. To the extent that this new view is well grounded in
reality, it can be communicated to others and readily understood.
Even Einstein's general theory of relativity, probably the most

profound creative idea yet experienced in human history, could be understood, if only by two or three other scientists then alive.

When the creative idea is not grounded sufficiently in reality it becomes a vision that can only be imperfectly communicated, and when the idea is completely decoupled from reality it becomes the madness of the wide awake dreamer, the insane.

The creative artist and presumably the creative businessman work within and continuously revisit their genre making advances that are communicable, if not immediately acceptable. The perfection of the creative idea is in the way it deepens the view of all that has proceeded but violates nothing.

In the book Oremland develops the idea of the patron and the importance to the artist. In the business world patrons do not normally exist, yet I had one and found him to be singularly important. I am not confusing the role of patron with that of the mentor. Indeed, I have been extremely fortunate to have had as mentors both David Packard and William Hewlett. The patron in my case was the Pittsburgh industrialist Henry Hillman. When I decided to become a full-time career venture capitalist, after some success as both a business manager and inventor-entrepreneur, it was Henry Hillman who decided to back me financially and who contributed over 50 percent to my first fund. He lent me his credibility, enabling me quickly to raise the balance and reinforce my belief in my own ideas.

During the early years of the fund I interacted with Henry as Oremland has described the interaction between the artist and patron. Although he had no legal control over my activities, I found myself frequently checking my scope, as I have defined it, with him. At the beginning I had told him that I could not predict what I might do, but that certainly I would not start another computer company. When later this is what I did do, I first reviewed all my thinking with him. I believe that Henry also saw his role as that of patron. He derived, I believe, considerable pleasure from his indirect participation in the creation of exciting new companies in biotechnology, computer software, and instrumentation well beyond the financial rewards that accrued.

Oremland has taken an immense challenge in this book, for to delineate human creativity is to delineate the quintessential distinction between the human animal and the human being, and we can be both pleased and enlightened in his success. I found his carefully reasoned development of the analogy of the dream, of play, and of the artist's creativity to be accurate and revealing as it pertains to my own work. I thank him for these new insights and for the opportunity to interact with him.

The Author Responds

In inviting these responses, I suggested that these respondents compare their subjective experience regarding creativity to the ideas expressed in the book. I expected that they would use a different lexicon but had not expected that they would use many different lexicons reflecting the ecology in which their creativity manifests.

Taken in broad sweeps, there was a striking difference between the businessman and the director and the two plastic artists, the painter and the sculptor. The businessman and the director emphasized that in their situation a product is produced and brought in within budget generally in a large community of collaborative interaction. The plastic artists tend to operate more or less timelessly, although the sculptor, with great sensitivity, described how his ''public'' pieces continuously intersect with multiple external interferences. Yet the style of thought of all four remarkably resembled one another.

All four insisted that the creator must be the prime mover throughout the process. As the sculptor stated, ''The work must be continually in process and never leave the domain of one's control, even though every world through which the sculpture passes—the worlds of permits, officialdom, and architecture—conspires against the artist's concept and insists that the artistic process was complete at the end of the design state'' (p. 141).

Although not always clearly stated, all the respondents delineated similar and familiar progressions in creating. Although not necessarily in linear progression, they differentiated: (1) inspiration; (2) a phase of playing with concepts; and (3) a phase in which the emerging concept is shaped, worked with, and organized within internal and external requirements. Their subjective experience easily is translated into an ontogenetic recapitulation: self-object fusion, transitional exploration, and tertiary discursive object-related functioning. The tertiary phase is particularly well described by the director, "We all recognize that on some level great acting is un-self-conscious, yet paradoxically it requires enormous consciousness and technique to attain that level of un-self-consciousness" (p. 138).

Supporting the hypothesis that creating is a form of object relatedness, all related to what they produce as *objects* in the psychoanalytic sense. They talk about what they create as a person. The parallel to the child is obvious. As the sculptor said, "One notices the day when the work, which heretofore had been devouring, returns the effort. The work smiles and gives that power back again to the artist" (p. 144). The businessman in another context related that a common problem businessmen who create companies have is that the companies become "their baby" and that they find it hard to let go of them. The director, in discussing the end of the rehearsal period, noted a period of mourning for the director as he or she realizes that the actors and the play must be let go of to be on their own. She analogized this difficulty in letting go to the parent and the child.

The four respondents did not place the heavy emphasis on originality that I do. In fact, the painter suggested that a heavy emphasis on originality can destroy creativity. Although she was largely concerned with the contemporary commercial overvaluing of originality, her thoughts approach my attempt to distinguish the original from the idiosyncratic. Related to her concerns about the overemphasis on originality is the inhibiting effect on creativity of an overawareness of the "external audience." I believe her idea of the "new emblem" in important ways adds to my attempts to understand the characteristics of the masterpiece.

In her discussion of originality, the painter's *footprints in the sand* metaphor is moving and telling. Perhaps, the way I discuss originality overly carries the connotation of monumental. In fact I have in mind *little* moments of originality as beautifully exemplified by the director's "little" interaction with Harold Pinter when he asked her to add a line at a particular moment for a specific production of *The Birthday Party*, a play then already twenty-five years old. I believe her statement, "There is acting that *describes* experience and acting that *is* experience" (p. 138) is close to what I mean by originality.

Although he questioned the relation of my concept of masterpiece to the business world, the businessman provided an additional and compelling view of the masterpiece. He wrote, "The perfection of the creative idea is in the way it deepens the view of all that has proceeded but violates nothing" (p. 159). Despite his modesty, it seems to me that the way his financial restructurings spurred subsequent multiple replications, modifications, and spinoffs go a long way toward qualifying them as masterpieces.

The businessman and the sculptor strongly responded to ideas regarding the importance of an "other," the patron, in creativity. The businessman more than the others distinguished between mentor and patron. I believe the businessman most clearly approached the difference between an identificatory *object* and an *object* that functions as "transitional mother." In the sculptor, the father seemed to have been both an identificatory object and the "transitional mother." The absence of such emphases by the director and the painter, both females, may point to differences in the development of creativity in men and women, or it may be idiosyncratic to these two women.

The painter adds the art dealer to my list of modern day patrons. In an important way, she reminds us of the significant role art dealers play in protecting, promoting, and inhibiting creativity. In the art dealer, we can often see the transitional mother with a stable of creative individuals. Like the transitional mother, the art dealer may be crucial to the development of creativity as well as of a career. I have an idea that many art dealers easily will sense the parallel between mother and them in their relationships with artists.

The painter makes the interesting point that patrons, male and female alike, are more interested in male than female artists, perhaps a manifestation of the frequent and little acknowledged preference of mothers for the male child. She exposes the unfairness that exists regarding women artists' access to gallery and museum exhibitions. She suggests that there are some current shifts as women artists "demand to be taken seriously" and as women openly express more interest in the art of women and the specific meanings to be found in the art of women. Some of this idea of specificity in the art of women is illustrated in the director's fascinating description of her Greek Chorus finding their place in her production of *Hecuba*.

All of the respondents acknowledged the importance of the role of the unconscious in creativity. All talked about a sense of being carried, spoken through, being witness to, being the instrument of, and the sense of solutions coming fully formed. The businessman more than the others wrote about the sense of omnipotence, the feeling of "being correct," that often accompanies epiphany. References to the importance of dreams and the parallels between dreaming and creativity were frequently noted. "That is what is fascinating and wonderful about (dreams), how the world of the dream becomes entirely plastic and is molded to the deeper need for psychological consistency and 'perfection.' Similarly, the creative idea seems to mold and restructure previously perceived reality to a new deeper view and perfection" (p. 158).

All of the respondents liked the term *play* and used it widely to express the sense of experimentation and freedom that is characteristic of creativity. The director explicitly discussed the rehearsal process as a "free-form exploration" in which "entire playlets can emerge and subside in the space of moments each with its own coherence and integrity" (p. 132). The businessman elaborated effectively on the difference between play and games. As he wrote, in creativity, "The game becomes play with endless new vistas" (p. 157).

The sculptor noted a related quality, keenly developed in creative individuals, the ability to "recognize" significances in what is produced, a quality related to the creative individual's unusual ability to endow *things* with meaning. He, like the director, clearly recognized the place of "accidents" in creativity, sensed how complicated an "accident" is, and discussed how embracing (finding meaning within) creative people are of their "accidents."

More than the others, the sculptor described rituals and altered states of consciousness associated with creativity. As he wrote, "As I clear the saw table to begin the day, I touch and thereby automatically invest myself with a recitative of past concerns" (p. 145). None of these creative individuals talked directly about fetish related special objects or conditions associated with their creating, phenomena frequently found in the accounts of creative individuals. The absence in these responses may reflect the fact that "special conditions" are so a part of their creativity that they fail to be noted. Interviews might have revealed little and big "special conditions."

In these accounts rarely was there discussion of mothers. Only the businessman wrote that he might be attempting to provide the mother with what she always longed for and that was not fulfilled by his father. It might seem that this absence of centrality of the mother runs against my pivotal thesis, that creativity is primarily a continuing inner dialogue related to the mother of the transitional phase of development. I see the absence of mother in these accounts as confirmation of the thesis. In effect creative people do not talk about their mothers in this regard because they are in frequent inner contact with them.

This is not to say that in other contexts, especially in interviews, that these creative individuals would not have provided extensive accounts of the importance of their mothers in their development. Yet, I believe that skillful interviewing would differentiate the mother in continuing transitional functioning (the continuing inner dialogue) and the mother as differentiated object, as I was able to describe in the cases such as the actress Bette (see chapter 4).

As would be expected, the role children play in the lives of creative people split markedly on gender lines. The two men scarcely mentioned their children; the two women wrote extensively about the relation of their children to their creativity.

Both of the women, both mothers, made the important point that although there is much recognition of the conflict between being a mother and being creative, little is acknowledged regarding the inhibition of creativity that can come if a creative woman renounces motherhood in favor of being creative. The director, a mother of two young children, made special note of how enlivening and enriching rearing children is to creativity. Yet one cannot forget the renowned ceramicist Viola Frey's aphorism, ''You can't be a wife and an artist,'' but of course psychodynamically being a wife is vastly different from being a mother. It almost seems that the creative woman needs a wife. Obviously we are only beginning to plumb the vicissitudes of the primal relationship between creation and procreation. Interestingly, none of the respondents to any extent mentioned spouses, other than the sculptor who ascribed to his wife and family some patron functioning during his year of artistic search.

Strikingly neither the men nor the women objected to my thesis regarding the essential androgyny of creative people. I believe that the androgyny went unmentioned because it is integral to their sense of self.

The painter, who of the respondents is the most conversant with psychoanalysis, most clearly recognized and praised my attempt to wrest creativity from the psychopathological cast that it tends to assume in psychoanalytic writing. Like all the respondents she endorsed my distinction between talent and creativity. Each added qualities to further the distinction. The businessman noted that although talent can be developed, ''Creativity . . . can be nurtured but not engendered'' (p. 151). I especially like his using the word *nurtured*.

The painter noted the frequent fear that artists have of psychoanalysis, fear stemming from many sources including the unfortunate aftermath of poor psychoanalysis. On a deep level, most frequently the fear of psychoanalysis by creative people reflects the fear of losing a precious relationship. The psychoanalyst as transference object is perceived as a threat to the maintenance of the transitional mother. In skillful psychoanalysis, the psychoanalyst in transference essentially becomes a reincarnation of the transitional mother allowing and encouraging the new explorations. The transitional relationship is enhanced. Psychodynamically the psychoanalyst essentially becomes a patron. In poor psychoanalysis, the psychoanalyst becomes the mother attempting to move the artist into object-related functioning, often severely inhibiting the creativity. Fortunately for the creative individual, such psychoanalyses frequently reach a stalemate and the relationship ruptures. Unfortunately, artists who have suffered from such misguided psychoanalytic endeavors often join and substantiate the group who propagate the idea that psychoanalysis is antithetical to creativity.

I appreciate that these respondents eagerly embraced the project even though each expressed concern that their lack of conversance with psychoanalysis and the psychoanalytic lexicon would limit what they could say. Although only one is a writer, all wrote clearly and beautifully about their subjective experience, their art, and how they responded to various key elements of my propositions. All found new things in what I wrote and added much. I am pleased that they helped me better understand my ideas by presenting them in new ways.

References

Arieti, S. (1976), *Creativity, The Magic Synthesis*. New York: Basic Books.

Balliet, W. (1990), Profiles: Dizzy Gillespie. *The New Yorker*, Sept. 17:48–60.

Beauvoir, S. de (1949), *Le Deuxième Sexe*. Paris: Gallimard.

Breuer, J., & Freud, S. (1893–1895), Studies on Hysteria. *Standard Edition*, 2. London: Hogarth Press, 1955.

Breznitz, S. (1971), A critical note on secondary revision. *Internat. J. Psycho-Anal.*, 52:407–439.

Brook, P. (1987), *The Empty Space*. New York: Atheneum.

Campbell, J. (1971), *The Portable Jung*. New York: Viking Press.

Castoriadis, C. (1984), *Crossroads in the Labyrinth*, tr. K. Soper & M. Ryle. Cambridge, MA: MIT Press.

———— (1987), *The Imaginary Institution of Society*, tr. K. Blamey. Cambridge, MA: MIT Press.

Chamberlin, E. R. (1982), *The World of the Italian Renaissance*. London: George Allen & Unwin.

Condivi, A. (1553), *The Life of Michelangelo*, tr. A. S. Wohl. Baton Rouge: Louisiana State University Press, 1976.

Dotson, E. G. (1979), An Augustinian interpretation of Michelangelo's Sistine Ceiling. (Part I). *Art. Bull.*, 61:2, 223–256.

Durkheim, E. (1915), *The Elementary Forms of the Religious Life*. New York: Free Press/Macmillan, 1965.

Eissler, K. R. (1971), *Discourse on Hamlet and "Hamlet."* New York: International Universities Press.

Elkins, J. (1994), The failed and the inadvertent: Art history and the concept of the unconscious. *Internat. J. Psycho-Anal.*, 75:119–133.

Empson, W. (1947), *Seven Types of Ambiguity*. New York: New Directions.

Erikson, E. H. (1937), Configurations in play. *Psychoanal. Quart.*, 6:139–214.

167

——— (1954), The dream specimen of psychoanalysis. *J. Amer. Psychoanal. Assn.,* 2:5–56.

——— (1963), *Childhood and Society.* New York: W. W. Norton.

——— (1977), *Toys and Reason.* New York: W. W. Norton.

Erikson, J. (1982), Personal communication.

Ferenczi, S. (1912), To whom does one relate one's dreams? In: *Further Contributions to the Theory and Technique of Psychoanalysis.* New York: Basic Books, 1952, p. 349.

——— (1913), Stages in the development of the sense of reality. In: *Sex in Psychoanalysis.* New York: Basic Books, 1950, pp. 212–239.

Fisher, C. (1965), Psychoanalytic implications of recent research on sleep and dreaming, Part II, Implications for psychoanalytic theory. *J. Amer. Psychoanal., Assn.,* 13:271–303.

Freud, S. (1887–1902), *The Origins of Psychoanalysis.* New York: Basic Books, 1954.

——— (1893–1895), Studies on Hysteria. Standard Edition, 2:54–69. London: Hogarth Press, 1955.

——— (1900), The Interpretation of Dreams. *Standard Edition,* 4 & 5. London: Hogarth Press, 1953.

——— (1907), Delusions and dreams in Jensen's *Gradiva. Standard Edition,* 9:3–95. London: Hogarth Press, 1959.

——— (1910), Leonardo da Vinci and a memory of his childhood. *Standard Edition,* 11:59–137. London: Hogarth Press, 1957.

——— (1914), The Moses of Michelangelo. *Standard Edition,* 13:209–236. London: Hogarth Press, 1955.

——— (1920), Beyond the pleasure principle. *Standard Edition,* 18:7–64. London: Hogarth Press, 1955.

——— (1935), Letter to Percy Allen. In the possession of the author.

Gedo, J. (1970), Thoughts on art in the age of Freud. *J. Amer. Psychoanal. Assn.,* 18:219–245.

——— (1983), *Portraits of the Artist.* New York: Guilford.

——— (1989), A psychoanalyst's response. In: *Michelangelo's Sistine Ceiling: A Psychoanalytic Study of Creativity,* J. Oremland. Madison, CT: International Universities Press, pp. 133–151.

Gedo, M. (1980), *Picasso: Art as Autobiography.* Chicago: University of Chicago Press.

Gilot, F., with Lake, C. (1964), *Life with Picasso.* New York: McGraw-Hill.

Goethe, J. W. (1795), Wilhelm Meister's apprenticeship. In: *Hamlet Enter Critic,* ed. C. Sacks & E. Whan. New York: Appleton-Century-Crofts, 1960.

Gombrich, E. (1954), Psycho-analysis and the history of art. *Internat. J. Psycho-Anal.*, 35:401–411.

―――― (1963), *Meditations on a Hobby Horse*. London: Phaidon.

Goodwin, D. K. (1994), The home front. *The New Yorker*, August 15:38–61.

Graves, R. (1948), *The White Goddess*. New York: Farrar, Straus, & Giroux, 1966.

Greenacre, P. (1957), The childhood of the artist. *The Psychoanalytic Study of the Child*, 12:47–72. New York: International Universities Press.

Grimm, H. (1900), *Life of Michel Angelo*, 2 Vols. New York: Greenwood Press.

Gruber, H. E. (1989), The evolving systems approach to creative work. In: *Creative People at Work*, ed. W. B. Wallace & H. E. Gruber. New York: Oxford University Press, pp. 3–24.

Hamburger, M., Ed. & Tr. (1952), *Beethoven: Letters and Journals, and Conversations*. New York: Pantheon.

Hawkins, D. R. (1966), A review of psychoanalytic dream theory in the light of recent psychophysiological studies of sleep and dreaming. *Brit. J. Med. Psychol.*, 39:85–104.

Hibbard, H. (1974), *Michelangelo*. New York: Harper & Row.

Jones, E. (1949), *Hamlet and Oedipus*. New York: W. W. Norton.

Kagan, J. (1984), *The Nature of the Child*. Cambridge, MA: Harvard University Press.

―――― Kearsley, R. B., & Zelazo, P. R. (1979), *Infancy: Its Place in Human Development*. Cambridge, MA: Harvard University Press.

Kernberg, O. (1968), The treatment of patients with borderline personality organization. *Internat. J. Psycho-Anal.*, 49:600–619.

―――― (1975), *The Borderline Conditions and Pathological Narcissism*. New York: Aronson.

Kohut, H. (1960), Beyond the bounds of the basic rule. *J. Amer. Psychoanal. Assn.*, 8:567–586.

―――― (1966), Forms and transformations of narcissism. *J. Amer. Psychoanal. Assn.*, 14:243–272.

―――― (1971), *The Analysis of the Self*. New York: International Universities Press.

Kramrisch, S. (1981), *Manifestations of Shiva*. Philadelphia: Philadelphia Museum of Art.

Kris, E. (1952), *Psychoanalytic Explorations in Art*. New York: International Universities Press.

Kuhns, R. (1983), *Psychoanalytic Theory of Art*. New York: Columbia University Press.

Lewin, B. D. (1948), Inferences from the dream screen. *Internat. J. Psycho-Anal.*, 29:224–231.

———— (1953), Reconsideration of the dream screen. *Psychoanal. Quart.*, 22:174–199.

Liebert, R. S. (1982), *Michelangelo*. New Haven, CT: Yale University Press.

Loewald, H. W. (1988), *Sublimation: Inquiries into Theoretical Psychoanalysis*. New Haven, CT: Yale University Press.

Lubin, A. (1976), Mysticism and creativity. In: *Mysticism: Spiritual Quest or Psychic Disorder?* Group for the Advancement of Psychiatry, Report 9:787–798.

McDonald, M. A. (1970), Transitional tunes and musical development. *The Psychoanalytic Study of the Child*, 25:503–520. New York: International Universities Press.

MacGregor-Hastie, R. (1988), *Picasso's Women*. Luton, Beds, U.K.: Lennard.

McGuire, W., Ed. (1974), *Freud–Jung Letters: The Correspondence Between Sigmund Freud and C. G. Jung*. Princeton, NJ: Princeton University Press.

Nash, S. (1994), Continuing the Serra debate. Open Forum. *The San Francisco Chronicle*, June 15.

Noy, P. (1968), The development of musical ability. *The Psychoanalytic Study of the Child*, 23:332–347. New York: International Universities Press.

———— (1994), How music conveys emotion. In: *Psychoanalytic Explorations in Music*, ed. S. Feder, R. L. Karmel, & G. Pollock. Madison, CT: International Universities Press.

Oremland, J. (1975), An unexpected result of the analysis of a talented musician. *The Psychoanalytic Study of the Child*, 30:375–407. New Haven, CT: Yale University Press.

———— (1978), Michelangelo's *Pietàs*. *The Psychoanalytic Study of the Child*, 33:563–591. New Haven, CT: Yale University Press.

———— (1980), Mourning and its effect on Michelangelo's art. *The Annual of Psychoanalysis*, 8:317–351. New York: International Universities Press, 1981.

———— (1983), Death and transformation in *Hamlet. Psychoanal. Inq.*, 3:485–512.

———— (1984), Empathy and its role in the appreciation of art. In: *Empathy*, Vol. 1, ed. J. Lichtenberg, M. Bornstein, & D. Silver. Hillsdale, NJ: Analytic Press, pp. 239–265.

———— (1985), Review of Laurie Wilson, *Louise Nevelson: Iconography and Sources. Psychoanalytic Perspectives on Art*, 1:323–332.

——— (1989), *Michelangelo's Sistine Ceiling: A Psychoanalytic Study of Creativity.* Madison, CT: International Universities Press.

——— (1990), The origins and dynamics of creativity: A psychoanalytic perspective. *Bull. Assn. Child Psychotherapists*, 8:4–9.

——— (1994), Talent and creativity. In: *The Spectrum of Psychoanalysis: Essays in Honor of Martin S. Bergmann*, ed. A. K., & A. D. Richards. Madison CT: International Universities Press, pp. 297–320.

Ostwald, P. (1985), *Schumann: The Inner Voices of a Musical Genius.* Boston: Northeastern University Press.

——— (1991), *Vaslav Nijinsky: A Leap into Madness.* New York: Lyle Stuart/Carol.

Panofsky, E. (1939), *Studies in Iconology.* New York: Oxford University Press.

——— (1955), Iconography and iconology: An introduction to the study of Renaissance art. In: *Meaning in the Visual Arts.* Garden City, NY: Doubleday/Anchor Books, pp. 26–54.

Piaget, J. (1945), *Play, Dreams and Imitation in Childhood.* New York: W. W. Norton, 1951.

Pollock, G. H. (1975), Mourning and memorialization through music. *The Annual of Psychoanalysis*, 3:423–436. New York: International Universities Press.

Poskitt, J. (1987–1988), Program notes. San Francisco Symphony, 76th Season, 1987–1988.

Prosser, E. (1971), *Hamlet and Revenge.* Stanford: Stanford University Press.

Reiser, M. (1994), Wagner's use of the leitmotif to communicate understanding. In: *Psychoanalytic Explorations in Music*, ed. S. Feder, R. L. Karmel, & G. Pollock. Madison, CT: International Universities Press.

Richardson, J. (1991), *A Life of Picasso*, Vol. 1. New York: Random House.

Ricoeur, P. (1970), *Freud and Philosophy: An Essay on Interpretation*, tr. D. Savage. New Haven, CT: Yale University Press.

Rose, G. J. (1978), The creativity of everyday life. In: *Between Reality and Fantasy*, ed. S. Grolnick & L. Barkin. New York: Jason Aronson, pp. 347–362.

——— (1980), *The Power of Form.* New York: International Universities Press.

Schapiro, M. (1956), Leonardo and Freud. *J. Hist. Ideas*, 17:147–178.

Shakespeare, W. (1600), *Hamlet*, ed. C. Hoy. New York: W. W. Norton, 1960.

Sharpe, E. F. (1959), *Dream Analysis*. London: Hogarth Press.

Sinding-Larsen, S. (1969), A re-reading of the Sistine Ceiling. *Acta ad Archaeologiam et Artium Historiam Pertinentia* (Institutum Romanum Norwegiae), 4:143–157.

Snyder, F. (1968), Toward an evolutionary theory of dreaming. *Amer. J. Psychiatry*, 123:121–135.

Stassinopoulos, A. (1988), *Picasso, Creator and Destroyer*. New York: Random House.

Steinberg, L. (1984), Review of Robert Liebert's *Michelangelo. NY Rev. Books*, 31/11:p. 18.

Steinmann, E. (1906), *Die Sixtinische Kapelle*, Vol. 3. München: F. Bruckmann.

Stern, D. N. (1985), *The Interpersonal World of the Infant*. New York: Basic Books.

Strindberg, A. (1888), Creditors. In: *Pre-Inferno*, tr. W. Johnson. New York: W. W. Norton, 1970, pp. 143–187.

Thomas, D. (1951), Notes on the art of poetry. In: *A Garland for Dylan Thomas*, ed. G. J. Firmage. New York: Clarke & Way, 1963.

Tolnay, C. de (1970), *The Tomb of Julius II*. Princeton, NJ: Princeton University Press.

———— (1975), *Michelangelo, Sculptor, Painter, Architect*. Princeton, NJ: Princeton University Press.

Trietler, L. (1994), Reflections on the communication of affect and idea through music. In: *Psychoanalytic Explorations in Music,* ed. S. Feder, R. L. Karmel, & G. Pollock. Madison, CT: International Universities Press.

Ulrich, A. (1989), Image profile. *Image*, Oct. 15:34–39.

Webster, P. D. (1948), Arrested individuation or the problem of Joseph and Hamlet. *Amer. Imago*, 5:225–245.

Whitebook, J. (1994), Sublimation—A frontier concept. In: *The Spectrum of Psychoanalysis: Essays in Honor of Martin S. Bergmann*, ed. A. K. & A. D. Richards. Madison CT: International Universities Press, pp. 321–336.

Wilson, L. (1981), *Louise Nevelson: Iconography and Sources*. New York: Garland.

Winnicott, D.W. (1953), Transitional objects and transitional phenomena. *Internat. J. Psycho-Anal.*, 34:89–97.

———— (1967), The location of cultural experience. *Internat. J. Psycho-Anal.*, 48:368–372.

———— (1971), *Playing and Reality*. New York: Basic Books.

Wölfflin, H. (1968), *Classic Art*, tr. P. & L. Murray. London: Phaidon.

Wysuph, C. L. (1970), *Jackson Pollock/Psychoanalytic Drawings*, Lt. 1941, Op. 28. New York: Horizon Press.

Index

Titles of illustrations and the page numbers on which they appear are in italic.

abandonment, 118
  feeling of, 90
abhorrence, 117
abilities, 151
  special, 79
  unusual, 80
abstract art, 40
abstraction(s), 40, 48
  vague, 87
absurdity, Wittgensteinian, 140
Academie Goncourt, 127
Academy, French, 127
acceptability, social, 93, 94
accident(s), 133, 145, 164
accomplice, silent, 69
accomplishments, 74
accounting, 153, 154
achievement(s), 74, 156
Achilles, 135
acrobat, 128
acting, 52, 65, 70, 76
acting-out, 33, 77
activities, 84
  enactment, 93
  higher order defensive, 107
actor (actress), 43, 56, 65–70, 78, 79,
    80, 131–134, 137–139, 155, 161,
    165
actuality(ies), 71
  historical, 2
Adam, 25
Adler, A., 18

Adolph, 145
admiration, ambivalent, 117
adolescence, 57, 62
adornment, personal, 136
adventures, romantic, 129
aegis, 84
  protective, 56, 73, 80
affection, 156
agency
  government, 96
  internalizing, 94
agent(s), 76, 85
  external, 83, 84
AIDS (acquired immunodeficiency
    syndrome), 109
alchemy, 41, 93
Allen, P., 168
alone, 99
  fears of being, 80
aloneness, 96
alterations, 85
altercations, 78
alternates, collective, 87
ambiguity(ies), xii, 25–28, 35–37, 43,
    137
ambition, 141
ambivalence(s), 80, 119–120, 149
American Conservatory Theater, 131
amulet, 92
analog, 158
analogy(ies), 30, 32, 43, 102, 123, 134,
    140, 151, 160

175

analysis
  iconographic, 5, 8, 9
  meta-iconographic, 6, 14, 22
  wild, 35
androgyny, 165
Anguissola, S., 128
anima/animus, 145
animal, human, 91, 160
annihilation, 44
Anonymous
  Alcoholics, 74
  Cocaine, 74
  Sex Addicts, 74
antagonism, 120
anthropology, 125
anxiety, 39, 44, 76, 123, 125, 130
  of aloneness, 55
  manic, 78
  primary, 55
  of separation, 56, 64
aphorism, 165
apparent, heir, 100
apology, potter's, 88
apotheosis, 42
architect(s), 47, 129
architecture, 46, 48, 129, 141, 160
Ardhanarisvara, 111, *112*
arenas, 144
Arieti, S., 33, 55, 95, 167
armature, 141
army, Greek, 135
arrogance, 158
art(s), xi, 24, 28, 29, 33, 34, 35, 37, 39,
    46, 48, 50, 83, 106, 124, 133, 144,
    147, 149, 158, 166
  abstract, 40, 43, 103
  as agent, 43, 49
  archetypal, 42
  "the art," 97
  attacks on, 44
  as biography, 53
  destruction of, 44
  evocation of, xiv, 24
  evocative power of, 40, 48
  father's, 120

  fear of, 49
  as form of object relatedness, 53
  fundamental purpose of, 106
  graphic, 79
  great, 49
  great works of, 41
  hack, 25
  kinesthetic, 43
  "my art," 89, 90
  as organizer, 43, 49
  performance, 151
  plastic, xi, 43
  propaganda, 25, 42
  provocative potential of, 43
  public, 142
  and religion, 93
  religious, 42
  school of dramatic, 66
  study of, xvi, 4, 21
  stuff of, 107
  unmoved by, 44
  visual, 128, 130, 151, 154
  of women, 163
  work of, xiii, 6, 124, 125
art appreciation, 27, 35, 36, 37, 38, 49,
    50, 101, 125
"Art, *Object,* and Personal Continuity,"
    106
artisans, 142
artist(s), 33, 34, 35, 38, 40, 41, 43, 44,
    46, 48, 51, 83, 86, 87, 89, 93, 97,
    101, 111, 123, 125, 128, 129, 137,
    142, 145, 151, 155, 157, 159, 161,
    163. 165, 166
  amateur, 74
  childhood of, 86
  collision of, 133
  con, 151
  creative, 157, 159
  decorative, 130
  fear of, 49
  fellow, 144
  female, 129, 130, 163
  graphic, 78
  great, 124

hack, 132
interpersonal world of, 86
jazz, 104
male, 129, 130, 163
modern, 140
out-of-town, 144
pejorative labels of, 87
performance, 151
performing, 132
plastic, 43, 160
in politics, 104
psychoanalytic work with, xi
relationship to their art, 51, 86
repetitive, 130
study of, xv, xvi, 4, 9, 16, 22
as teachers, 34
visual, 151
women, 129
artist, the, xi
"Art's Provocative Potential," 43–49
ascent of humankind, 111, 114
Ashmolean Museum, Oxford, 14, 16
ashrams, 74
aspirations, 124
assault(s), 71, 154
assistants, 118
association(s), 36, 74
   dreamer's, 36
   free, 27
   trivial or portentous, 88
   word, 27
assurance, 156
asymmetries, 40, 103
attitude, antielitist, 47
audience, 27, 38, 67, 80, 86, 88, 134,
       136, 138
   actual, 102, 139
   dialogue with, 102
   external, 161
   live, 139
   "unseen," 101, 102, 139
Austen, J., 127
author, 124, 133
autobiography, xvi
autogestation, 111

autoinsemination, 111
autonomy, 39
avatar, 96
awareness, 92, 94, 134

Bach, J. S., 71, 156
Baker, K., 46
ballerina, 72
Balliet, W., 104, 166
bankers, 124
Barkin, L., 171
bas-reliefs, 144
beauty, 140
   classical, 47
   despoiled, 48
Beauvoir, S. de, 126, 127, 167
Beaux, C., 128
Beethoven, L. van, 71, 103
being, 52, 106, 117
   human, 91, 160
   living, 118
Bell, V., 129
benefits, tax, 154
bereavement, xv
Berlin, 99
Berry, W., 149
Bette, 79, 165
   See also case illustrations
Beyond the Pleasure Principle, 54
Bible, The, 7
biography, 4, 22, 51, 139
   depth, xvi
birth, 39, 42, 52
Birthday Party, The, 137, 162
Bishop, L., 129
biunity, 114
   primal, 111, 117
Blamey, K., 167
blanket, 32, 90
blindness, hysterical, 1–3
blocking, 72
blues, 57, 62
body(ies), 39, 60, 72, 73, 80
   dead, 66
   expressiveness, 72

grotesquely feminized, 62
molding, 73
mother's, 32, 102, 103
natural language of, 128
symmetry of, 103
Bonheur, R., 128
Bosnia, 135
boundaries, 134, 157
Bourgeois, L., 129
bourgeoisie, ascendancy of the, 128
boys, beautiful, 110
Bradshaw, J., 73, 74, 77
braggadocio, 74
brain, 30, 124
break, paranoid, 68
breakthroughs, creative, 135
breast, 40, 84, 103
Brecht, B., 138
Breughels, the, 124
Breuer, J., 1, 2, 167
Breznitz, S., 24, 167
British Museum, Trustees of, 113
Brontë
   sisters, 124
   Emily, 127
Brook, P., 132, 167
Brooks, R., 128
budget, 134, 155, 160
Buonarroto, M. *See* Michelangelo
business, 30, 104, 140, 151, 154, 155,
   157, 158
businesspeople (businessman), 43, 83, 151–
   160, 161, 163–164, 165

calling, inner, 130
Calling of Matthew, The, 42
Campbell, J., 93, 167
capacity(ies), 52
   defensive and its place in talent, 81
   divine, 52
   internalizing, 53, 95
   to relate, 106
capital, venture, 153
capitalist, venture, 159
Caravaggio, 42

career, 70, 71, 141, 153, 163
*Cartoon for Madonna with St. John and
   St. Anne,* 10, *13*
Casadesus, the, 124
case illustrations
   Bette, 65–70
   Edward, 97–99
   James, 72–73
   Mr. Z., 70–72
   Pete, 73–79
   Tom, 56–65
Cassatt, M., 128
cast, psychopathological, 165
Castoriadis, C., 30, 93, 94, 123, 167
castration, 63, 64
catastrophe, 68
Caterina, 12, 14
catharsis, subjective, 125
Cecchino, 110
celebrities, 109
cello, 88
centrality, 164
   psychical, 119
ceramicist, 165
Chamberlin, E. R., 96, 167
chance, 145
character(s), 69, 94, 127, 131, 133, 139
   fictional, xiv, 42
characteristics, common, 156
charger, 6–8
Chekhov, A., 131
Chevalier de la Legion d'Honneur, 123
child(ren), 61, 69, 90, 93, 97, 106, 117–
      119, 129, 134, 138–140, 144, 156,
      161, 165
   adult, 119–120
   of creative men, 120
   of creative women, 119
   gifted, 99
   inner, 77
   male, 130, 163
   newborn, 117
   observation of, 32
   transitional, 70
childhood, 14, 62, 156

"Childhood of the Artist, The," 86
choice, object, 110
    See also object and *object*
choreographers, 134–135
choreography, 127
Chorus, the, 135–136
    Greek, 163
Church, the, 126
Churchill, W., 104
classes, acting, 76
classmates, 75, 76
Claudius, King, xiii
Cliché des mesée nationaux (The Louvre, Paris), 10, 11, 12
clothing, 136
clowning, 74
clubs, 76
Colette, 127
collaboration, 134
collaborators, group of, 132
colleagues, 97, 128
color(s), 40, 85, 86, 104
comedian, 56, 73
comedy, 66
comic, 76, 79, 81
Commander dans L'Order des Arts et Lettres, 123
commission, 29, 41, 134
commitment, 65
commonalities, 24
communication, 27, 31, 91, 93, 137
    need for, 105
    singular, 25
community, 144
    art, 48
company(ies), 154, 155, 161
    ballet, 72
    biotechnology (genetic engineering), 153
    computer, 159
    repertory theater, 65, 66, 69
compartmentalization, 42
compensation, defensive, 118
competition(s), 120, 140, 141, 155
    conscious and unconscious, 97

competitors, dangerous, 130
complement, volumetric, 80
complex, sociopsychophysiological, 84
composer(s), 44, 70, 71, 129, 134, 135, 146
composites
    integrated, 92
    multilayered, 101
composition(s), 56, 57, 64, 70, 94
compromises, 81
compulsion, 124
    to repeat (repetition compulsion), 54
computer, rudimentary, 98
concept
    artist's, 141, 160
    energic, 93
    generic, 85
    initial, 154
    integrated differentiated, 85
    new, 126
    playing with, 161
concerts, 70
condensation, xii, 8, 23–26, 28, 36, 41, 43, 75, 142
    and ambiguity, 25–28
conditions, special, 164
Condivi, A., 18, 167
conductor(s), 43, 71
confession, 74
confidant, 99
confidence, 158
configuration(s), 86, 99, 142
conflation of talent and creativity, 52, 53, 55
conflict(s), 40, 79, 165
    inner, 124
    intergenerational competitive, 100
    neurotic, 80
    oedipal, 72, 80
    resolution of, 92
confrontation(s), 157
    visual, 68
connectedness, 139
connection, spontaneous, 138
connotations, 83

conscience, 119
conscious and unconscious, 26, 33, 41
consciousness, 94, 138, 161
  altered states of, 164
consistency
  inner, 38
  psychological, 158, 163
constellations
  defensive, 53, 94
  enduring, 84
constitutions, political, 94
constraints, academic, 128
construct
  metapsychological, 83
  rickety, 149
consummation, height of, 117
contempt, 56, 58, 62
content(s), 80, 97
  artistic, 51, 53
  of creativity, 53, 54
  latent, 9, 28
  psychic, 4
  psychoanalytic study of, 86
  social acceptability of, 94
contention, bone of, 62
context, 142
contiguity, 91
continuance, artist's, 117
continuances, intrapsychic, 54
continuation, sole, 116
continuity(ies), 84, 91, 117, 146
  desire for, xii
  personal, 106
continuum, 54, 126
contortions, facial, 75
contributor, 157
controversy, 47
conversation, 74, 101
conviction, 37
Coronation of Napoleon, The, 42
*Corregidor/Bataan National Monument,
  The,* 140
correspondence, 99, 127
  Jung-Freud, 100
Cosmos, 142, *143,* 144

craftspeople, 88
crazy, 62, 98
creating, 54, 151
creation(s), 63, 145, 147, 165
  internal, 95
  limitless, 95
  pictorialization of, 111
creativity, xv, 30, 33, 51–56, 69, 71, 73,
      79–80, 90, 95, 97, 99, 105–106,
      110–111, 114, 116–121, 123–
      125, 129, 130–131, 132, 134,
      137–142, 144, 146, 147, 149, 151,
      153, 156–158, 160–165
  affinity with homosexuality, 109
  alternative to loving, 53
  applications of psychoanalysis to study
      of, 4
  characteristic of, 93
  as defensive, xii
  development of, 55, 90
  dynamics of, 52, 90
  enhanced psychoanalysis by, 81
  exploration of talent and, 80
  female, 121
  a form of relating, xii
  fundamentals of, 120
  genesis of, 90
  impingement, 71, 73
  inhibition of, 56, 64, 71, 165
  and madness, 98
  mother's, 120
  nascent, 114
  and 'object' relatedness, 83–86
  origins of, xvi, 4, 53, 90
  parallel to play, 54
  parent's, 120
  pregender roots, 121
  primal, 111, 117
  psychoanalytic study(ies) of, xiv, 3, 14,
      51, 65, 91–92
  psychodynamics of, xvi, 53, 95, 98
  and relatedness, 83–107
  relation to ontogeny, 85
  relation to procreation, 117
  relation of talent and, 79

relation of women to, 117
and sexuality, 109–121
spirit of, 54
subjective experience of, 33
talent as a defense against, 55, 151
women's, 126
creator, 134, 136, 160
Creditors, The, 145
cries, orgiastic, 58
critic, the, 46, 130
didactic, 145
fear of, 102
culture, 3, 43, 116
curator, chief, 47, 48
curiosity(ies), infantile, 2
cycle
dream, 31
feeding, 31
impossible, 156

dance, 23, 44, 52, 62, 103, 109
dancer(s) 43, 44, 79, 80
ballet, 56
principal, 72
daughter, 14, 135
David, J. L., 42
dealer
antique, 65
art, 130, 162–163
death(s), xv, 39, 42, 109
*Debate Between Madness and Love,
The,* 126
debates, 104
Decalogue, 18
decapitation, 7, 8
decay, 48
decoding, 33
dedifferentiation
gender, 120
regressive, 103
of self and nonself, 105
of self and *object,* 98
of the sensory modalities, 103
defamiliarization, 140
defense(s), 85, 94, 125

hierarchical view of, 95
higher level, 81, 95
higher order, 95
low-level, 80, 81
definition, 85
Degas, E., 128
Delauny, S., 129
delay, 84
Demetrios, A., 140–51, *143, 148, 150,
152*
demonstrations, 67
denial, 94
dependency, 39
depiction, 22, 51
character, 26
male artists', 127
depression, 56, 60, 63, 65, 71, 119
deprivation, 84
designers, set and lighting, 134, 135
desire(s), 31, 131
guilt-laden, 2
incestuous exhibitionistic, 62
incoherent, 124
overwhelming, 124
promiscuous, 61
universal to return to mother, 14
despair, 76, 140
destiny, 129, 147
destroyer, 145
destruction, 145, 147
detachment, 156, 157
deterioration, physical and mental, 59
developer, land, 144
development, 84
of creativity, 86
expensive, 153
heterosexual, 121
device, 154
competitive, 155
imaging, 155
dew, Eden's, 88
Diadkine, R., 123
dialectic, 33, 39
God-humankind, 92
dialogue, 17, 38, 69, 80, 101, 102, 144,
147

inner, xii, 28, 70, 81, 133, 164, 165
dichotomy, 33
  conscious-unconscious, 134, 149
difference, gender, 126
differentiation, 85, 91
  emerging of self and nonself, 105
  gender, 116
  transitional, 103
dimension, 9, 16
direction, 146, 153
  stage, 137
director, 68–70, 131–140, 160, 161, 162,
       163, 164, 165
  creative, 132
  film, 154–156
  hack, 132
  stage, 131
disability, learning, 74
disappointment, 90, 146
disarticulations, 54
disasters, 142
discards, 145
discipline, lack of, 76
disclosure, total, 125
discourse, discursive, 33
Discourse on Hamlet and "Hamlet," xiv
discovering, initial, 92
disease, 42
  Tourette's, 75
diseases of nose, throat, and ears, 99
distance, 76
distinction, 160
distortion, 85
Divine, the, 95, 111, 114
divorce, 120
documentation, 99
domesticity, simple, 118
Dona Albiera, 12
Dotson, E. G., 37, 38, 167
drama
  American, 43
  interpersonal, 101
  sadomasochistic, 67
dream, xiii, xvi, 23–25, 28–29, 33, 36,

38, 43, 50, 53, 55, 89, 90, 95, 102,
       123, 135, 147, 151, 158, 160, 163
  and communication, 31–32
  content of, 24
  disdain for, 44
  exploration of, 107
  externalized, 30, 149
  formation of, 23
  interpretation of one's own, 35
  Lewin's model, 40
  structure and formation, 51
  trombone dream(s), 59, 62
  two-leveled structure of, 32
  understanding of, 1
dreamer, 36, 37, 38, 159
dreaming, xii, 31, 32, 54, 55, 151, 163
drive, 55, 83, 84
drop (negative space), 147, 149
drug(s), 59, 74
duality(ies), 147, 149, 157
Duchamp, M., 41
Duncan, I., 127
duplicity, 135
Durkheim, E., 92, 125, 167
dyad, Michelangelo–Julius, 101
dyadic and monadic. *See* monadic and
       dyadic
Dynasty, Chola, 112
dysymmetries, 40

ear, 124
Earth, 126
ecology, 160
ecstasy, 42, 146
education, 79, 146, 151
egg
  cosmic, 126
  fertilized, 111
ego, 94, 158
Eiffel Tower, 42
einfülung (German), 50
Einstein, A., 158
Eissler, K. R., xiv, 167
elaboration, retrospective, 85
elements, 49

elite, rich, 47
Elkins, J., 33, 167
Elliot, G., 127
embellishments, 56, 71
emblem, new, 126, 162
embodiment, 111
emotion, 44, 129, 138, 139
empathy, 50
Empson, W., 26, 167
Empty Space, The, 132
enacting, transitional, 64
enactments, 1, 54, 70, 110
    autoplastic, 55
    external, 55
    mastery, 93
endings, happy, 66, 67, 70
endowment, innate extraordinary sensori-
        motoric-conceptual, 52, 86, 87
energy
    creative, 145
    psychic, 93
engineers, 155
entities, intrapsychic, 84
envy, 118
epiphany, 134, 146, 163
epoch, 3, 43, 49, 96, 116
era, depression, 156
erections, 60
Erikson, E. H., 32, 54, 55, 102, 117, 167
Erikson, J., 88, 167
ethnography, 125
ethos, 41
Euripides, 135
evaluation, personality, 27
events
    alloplastic, 55
    archetypical, 3
    creative, 132
    historical, 4
    internal, 55, 91
    intrapsychic, 54
    personal, 3
    physiological, 84
    school, 76
    topical, 3

evil, 147
evocation, 51
evolution, 92
exaggerations, repetitive, 81
excitement, 157
exhibitionism, 62
exhibitions, 163
existence, 94, 124
    Bohemian, 129
exit, 67, 137
expectation, internal and external, 119
experience(s) (ing), 138, 155, 162
    aesthetic, 53
    childhood, 140
    internalized, 84
    interpersonal, 50
    mystical, 105
    play with, 105
    subjective, 160, 161, 166
    transitional, 93, 105
    universal, 39, 40
    visual, 40
experimentation(s), 54, 163
explication, 36
explicitness, degrees of, 101
exploration, 70, 80, 96, 124, 132, 133,
        163
    child's, 140
    of the dream, 107
    kinesthetic, 103
    new, 166
    transitional, 161
exposition of art
    psychoanalytic, xiv
expression, 87, 128
    creative, 118
    disguised, 80
    external, 107
    liberation of, 124
    sources of, 106
    spontaneous, 138
externalizations, 70
extraneousnesses, 28, 37
eye(s), 70, 103, 124
eye to eye, 40

eyesore, 48

fabrication, 142
face(s), 74–75
  mother's, 39, 40, 103
  primal, 40
"Failed and the Inadvertent, The: Art
    History and the Concept of the
    Unconscious," 33
Falstaff, 42
family, 62, 76, 120, 125, 146, 165
  aristocratic, 128
  dysfunctional, 77
  Noah's, 111
fantasy(ies), 9, 10
  epicene, 111
  impossible, 100
father(s), 57, 58, 59, 62, 63, 65, 66, 67,
    69, 71, 72, 73, 74, 75, 76, 77, 78,
    79, 98, 117, 121, 124, 128, 140,
    141, 156, 162, 164
  absences, 60
  creative, 119
  vanquished, 80
fear(s) 39, 70, 129, 130, 166
  castration, 8
  neurotic, 80
Feder, S., 171, 172
feeling, oceanic, 105
female(s), 62, 120, 121, 129, 147, 162
  masculinized, 111
femaleness, fluid sense of, 110
feminine, 61, 110
femininity, 111, 120
Ferenczi, S., 25, 31, 167
fertility, mother's, 117
fetish, 92, 164
fiddle, second, 120
field(s)
  commercial, 153
  psychical, 93
  transitional, 93, 96
figure(s), 73, 147, 149
  alternative, 86
  mothering, 90

Fine Arts Museums of San Francisco,
    44, 46
fingerprint, 41
Fini, L., 129
finiteness, fear of, 106
Firmage, G., 172
Fisher, C., 31, 167
Flaubert, G., 127
Fliess, W., xiii, 99–100
fluidity
  gender, 111
  intrapsychic, 92, 110
  sense of, 33
Food and Drug Administration, 153
footprints, 125, 162
forces
  contradictory, 149
  countervailing, 158
  society limiting women and creativ-
    ity, 118
form(s), 53–54, 78, 80, 85, 107, 142, 149
  alternative, 86
  artistic, 51
  classical, 61
  connotative, 40
  hermaphroditic, 111
  jazz, 61
  poetic, 23
  psychoanalytic study of, 86
  pyramidal, 10
  two-headed maternal, 12
formation(s)
  of the art object, 107
  compromise, 1, 4, 51, 64, 69, 79
  of the dream, 30
  dream image, 24
  reaction, 53, 80, 81, 94
  symbol, 132
  symptom, 51, 54
formulations, 73
  psychopathological, 95
foundries, 141
fountain(s), 49, 146
  classical, 48
  undistinguished, 45

fragmentation, 149
Francis I of France, 126
Frank, R., 19
Fratelli Alinori, S. A. Rome, 15, 20
freedom, 54, 163
free will, 147
Freud, S., xv, 1, 2, 4, 6, 9, 10, 12, 13, 14,
        16, 18, 21, 23, 24, 25, 26, 27, 29,
        30, 31, 36, 37, 38, 39, 40, 51, 54,
        55, 83, 84, 85, 92, 93, 99–100,
        107, 146, 167, 168
    explorations of creativity, xii, xvi
    pathography. *See* pathography
Frey, V., 165
fulfillment(s), 90
    basic physiological need, 84
    wish, 54
fun, 147, 157
function(s)
    mothering, 90
    patron, 99
functioning, 105
    object related, 161, 166
    patron, 96, 100, 118, 165
    transitional, 32, 55, 56, 80, 81, 96, 97,
            105, 118, 120, 133, 165
fundament, 147
    presexual, maternal, 101
fusion
    primary, 103, 105
    self-object, 161

gain, capital, 154
Galileo, 126
galleries, art, 130, 163
Galton, F., 24, 27
gambling, 158
game(s), 54, 138, 157, 164
    dangerous, 58
Gedo, J., xvi, 53, 168
Gedo, M., xvi, 53, 168
generation(s), 124, 129
generativity
    human, 111, 114, 116
    parthenogenic version of object
            related, 117

genesis, 4, 21, 39, 90, 121
Genesis, 41
gender, 120, 129
genius, 124, 129
genre(s) 5, 6, 8, 28, 44, 105, 159
Gentileschi, A., 128
gift(s), 33, 34, 89, 104
gifted, less, 85, 86, 87, 90
gigs, 76
Gillespie, J. B., 104, 167
Gilot, F., 118, 123–131, 168
girls, 57, 62
God, 33, 92
    breasted, androgynic, 111
God given, 33
Goddess, White, 90, 117
Goethe, J. W., xiv, 168
Gogh, T. van, 97
Gogh, V. van, xvi
Golden Gate Bridge, 45, 46
Gombrich, E., 9, 169
Goncharova, N., 128
Gonzalez, E., 128
Goodwin, D. K., 104, 198
Gradiva, 26
graduation, 76
graffiti, 48
Graham, M., 127
grandparents, 120
granite, 154
gratification, 87
Graves, R., 90, 97, 117, 118, 169
Greece, 126, 135
Greek, 149
Greenacre, P., 52, 83, 86, 87, 92, 169
Grimm, H., 18, 168
Grolnick, S., 171
groups, 76, 151
Gruber, H. E., 65, 169
guilds, 128, 140
guilt, 72
Gustav, 145

hack, 156

Haimovitz, M., 88
Halicarnassus, 101
Hamburger, M., 104, 169
Hamlet, xiii, xv, 26, 66
Hamlet and Oedipus, xiv
hand, 124, 145, 149, 151
Hanold, N., 26
harmony, 104
Hawkins, D. R., 31, 169
Hecuba, 135, 163
helplessness, 78
Heptameron, 126
Hepworth, B., 129
Hercules, 5
heredity, 33, 52
heritage, 146
hermaphroditism, 111
hero, 95, 128
heterosexuality, 110
Hewlett, W., 159
Hibbard, H., xiv, 100, 169
Hillman, H., 159
Hindu, 111
historian, art, 37, 38
Histories, Sistine Ceiling, 111
history, 156
 art, 4, 5, 8, 22, 48
 human, 159
Holofernes, 7
holon, 149
home, mental, 133
Home, 133
homeless, 48
homeostasis, 54
homosexuality
 affinity between homosexuality and
   creativity, 109
 female, 110
 Leonardo's, 10
 male, 110
hope(s), 140, 144
Hopkins, H., 104
Horse, Trojan, 135
hostility, 62, 69, 120
Hoy, C., 172

hubris, 117
humanity(ies), 6, 141
humankind, 41, 111
humiliation, 73
Humphrey, D., 127
hunch, gambler's, 158
husband(s), 119
hymns, mystical, 126
hysteria, 1

iconograph(s), 29
 personal, 6
iconography, 28
iconology, 5–6, 9
idea, 119
 of being understood, 100
 of breast, 84
 creative, 134, 158, 159, 163
 idiosyncratic, 99
 ingenious, 104
 new, 158
identification(s), 53, 79, 80, 81, 94, 95,
   109, 120
 with the aggressor, 78
identity, reborn ideal, 117
idiosyncrasy, 99
idiosyncratic, the, 161
Ignudi 114, *116*
illness, mental, 53
image(s), 6, 13, 14, 36–37, 43, 104, 126,
   134, 147, 149
 actualized, 38
 archetypal, 95
 art, xv, 5, 9, 27, 36
 body, 39, 119
 complex, 27
 condensed, 8, 24, 28
 dream, xv, 8, 24, 25, 27–28, 35, 36
 hermaphroditic, 116
 inner, 12
 mental, 38
 visual, 23, 40
imagery
 anal, 48
 hermaphroditic, 114

resonance of, 86
imagination, collective, 132
imitations, 75, 77
immortality, xii, 106, 117
immortals, 106
Impressionists, 128
improvisations, 71, 104, 134, 139
  solo, 58
  jazz, 64
inconsistencies, 37
  artistic, 18
incorporation, 80
individuals, creative, 85, 90, 156, 162, 164, 166
individuation, 64
inevitability, 146
infant(s), 31, 84, 96
infantile, 87
infidelities
  father's, 61
  fellow musicians', 61
  mother's, 61
ingénue, 65, 66, 69
inheritance, human ahistorical, 41
inhibition(s), 70, 71, 80, 130, 147, 165
  ego, 79
inkblot, 27
innate, 124
innovation, technical, 41
innuendo, coy, 69
"inrections," 60
inspiration, 29, 146, 161
  artistic, 125
  moments of, 103
  subjective, 64
instability, 40
installation, 142
institution, 96, 127, 130
instrument, 57, 59, 61, 63, 88, 163
  fetish quality to, 58
instrumentalist(s), 43, 44
instrumentation, 159
integration, 31, 54, 64, 85, 91, 126
  of narcissistic aspects of the personality, 53

integrity, 132, 163
  poetic, 90
intelligence, 98
intensity, masochistic, 110
interaction
  collaborative, 160
  little, 162
interchange(s), 78
  family, 76
interests, competing, 119
interferences, multiple external, 160
internalizations, 84
interpretation(s), 25, 49, 70, 71, 155
  art, 35, 36, 38
  biographical, 39
  clinical, 6
  complimentary, 38
  cultural, 39
  dream, 27, 35–38
  dyadic dream, 35
  historical, 39
  iconologic, 5, 6, 9
  interpreter's, 36
  meta-iconographic, 6, 13, 14
  Moses, 18
  pietá, 14
  psychoanalytic, 2, 4, 38, 39
  psychodynamic, 38
  social, 39
  unitary, 42
  validity of, 37
  verbalized, 38
Interpretation of Dreams, The, xiii, 23
interpreter(s), 35–37, 49
interrelatedness, 37, 49
interventions
  interpreter's, 36
  mystical, 52
interview(ing) (s), 164–165
intimidations, 65
introjection, 53
introjects, 27
introspection, 146
intuition, 5, 146
intuitive, 146

invention, 96, 154
  endless, 56
inventor-entrepreneur, 159
investor(s), 153, 154
  venture capital, 151
involution, 39, 42
Israelites, 18
issue(s), 106, 117
  nature-nurture, 118

jazz, 56, 57, 61, 62
jealousy, 90, 97, 118, 120
Jensen, W., 26
Jerusalem, new, 41
Jesus, 12, 25
Joan of Arc, 126
job, 78, 132
  director's, 134
John, G., 128
John, the Evangelist, 92
John the Baptist, 7
Johnson, W., 171
jokes, 76
Jones, E., xiv, 18, 21, 169
journeyman, 140, 146
Joyce, J., 86
Judith 6–8, *7*
Julius II, 21, 41
  and Michelangelo, 100–101
  as patron, 101
  as person, 100
  Tomb of, (the tragedy), 10, 101
Jung, C. G., 6, 18, 26, 27, 93, 99–100
junk, 46, 47, 48
justifications, valid, 142

Kagan, J., 85, 169
Kalho, F., 129
kare (Indo-European), 52
Karmel, R., 171, 172
Kauffman, A., 128
Kearsley, R. B., 85, 169
Kernberg, O., 95, 169
Kieffer, A., 42
king, Thracian, 136

King John, xv
King Lear, 43
Kitka, 135, 136
Kleiner, Perkins, Caufield & Byers, 151
knowledge, 124
  clairvoyant, 105
Koestler, A., 149
Kohut, H., 53, 92, 169
Köllwitz, K., 129
Kramrisch, S., 111, 112, 169
Krasner, L., 129
Kris, E., 33, 55, 92, 110, 169
Kuhns, R., 37, 54, 169

Labé, L., "La Belle Cordière", 126
Lacan, J., 123
La Cité des Dames, 126
La Fayette, M-M de, 127
Lake, C., 168
landscape, 136
Lang, D., 135
language, 138, 140
  private, 61
lasers, 154
latency, 62, 66
Laurencin, B., 129
law, business, 153
leader, business, 156
Leda, hemaphroditic, 111
Leda and the Swan, 111, *113*
Le Deuxième Sexe, 126
Legion of Honor, 44–45, 47
Lempicka, T. de, 129
lend-lease, 104
Leonardo, *See* Vinci, L. da
Les Demoiselles d'Avignon, 125
Letters by Marquise de Sevigné, 127
level(s)
  cognitive, 105
  psychical, 117
Levy-Bruhl, L., 125
Lewin, B. D., 32, 39, 40, 55, 102–103,
  170
lexicon, 160
  mechanistic, 83

psychoanalytic, 166
scientific, 33
Liebert, R. S., 100, 170
Liebovici, S., 123
life, 140, 142, 165
physical, 138
stage, 136
lifeless, 141
lifelong, 90
light, 42
line(s)
developmental, male and female, 121
gender, 165
lineage(s), family 53
link(s), mystical, 95
Linus, 32
literature, 26, 98, 126–127, 147
location
of creativity, 86, 89, 149
internal, 32
of play, 102
Loewald, H. W., 94, 170
logic, dream free-associative, 134
loneliness, 57, 59
longing, sense of, 131
loss early, 63
Louvre, 46
love, 87, 88, 106, 126, 145, 156
affair with the world, 92
enlightened, 130
fear of loss of, 64
idealized, 110
"my first love," 89, 132
"my love," 89
lover(s), 97, 118
Lubin, A., xvi, 170

MacGregor-Hastie, R., 97, 118, 170
McDonald, M. A., 44, 170
McGuire, W., 100, 170
madness, 98, 99, 105, 158, 159
madonna, 14
Madonna with Saint Anne, 14, *16*
maenad, 118
Maffei, F., 6, 7, 8, 9

magic, 95
magician, 95
maker, 144, 145
idol, 93
image, 140
malcontent, 67
male(s), 121, 129, 147
maleness, fluid sense of, 110
malignancy, 68
maltreatment, psychological and physical, 118
mammals, 31
man (men), 8, 65, 126, 129, 133, 149, 162, 165
creative, 117–119
descent of, 111
domesticated, 97, 117
old, 67
manager, business, 159
manifestation, 146, 163
mannerisms, 75, 77
mantras, 77
maquette, 44, 141, 146, 147
Marot, C., 126
masculinity, 61, 110–111
masochist, 65
masterpiece, 13, 28, 37–38, 40–43, 104, 125–126, 127, 147, 154, 155, 162
masters, 156
mastery, 39, 40, 51, 53, 54, 85, 92, 93, 107
masts, vertical, 142
material, 149
three-dimensional, 141
maternity, burden of, 129
matrix, 93
creative, 107
formal, 39
primal psychical, 85
self-nonself, 91
social, 3
underlying, 39
maturation, 84
maturity, sexual, 72
Mausolus, 101

meaning(s), 5, 21, 65, 84, 91, 164
  connotative, 107
  levels of, 26
  limitless, 43
  multiple, 38, 49
  new, 70
  of dreams, 54
  of symptoms, 54
  psychoanalytic view (understanding) of 1, 3
  singular, 79
  transcultural, 41
  transoceanic, 41
  visible, condensed, multiple, metaphoric, 24
Meaning in the Visual Arts, 5
mechanisms, dream, 23
Medici
  garden, 96
  Lorenzo, the Magnificent, 96
  Marie dei, 42
medium, 83, 124, 126
meetings, 157
memory(ies), 9, 70, 85
  cherished, 63
  childhood, xv
  vivid, 54
mentor, 96, 124, 159, 162
merger
  self and *object,* 105
  self-nonself, 105
meta-autobiography, xvi
metabiography, xvi, 4, 9, 22
metaphor, 89, 114, 120, 125, 138, 162
  depth, 2, 24
metapsychology, xvi, 6, 83
method, 38, 146
Method, The, 139
methodology of psychoanalysis, 21
Michelangelo, xi, 6, 21, 41, 43, 51, 100–101, 111, *113–116*
  drawing, 14
  idealized love of Cecchino, 110
  life and art of, 110
  See also Leda and the Swan, Sistine

Chapel Ceiling.
Middlemarch, 127
Mill on the Floss, The, 127
mimic, 77
mind, 6, 30, 104, 145
  popular, 98
  undisciplined, 105
mirrors, interferometer, 154
mistresses, 118
mistrust, 120
modality(ies)
  art, 23
  kinesthetic, 23
  new, 42
  sensory, 52
mode, social acceptability of, 94
model(s), 97
  drive, 83
  nude, 128
  topographic, 33
Modersohn-Becker, P., 128
Moillon, L., 128
Mona Lisa, 10, *12*
monadic and dyadic, 33, 36, 38
monologue, 27, 28
  inner, 101, 139
moon, hidden side of, 130
Morisot, B., 128
"Moses" of Michelangelo, The, 16, 18, 20, 21, 22, 36, 38–39, 40, 146
mother(s) 12–14, 31–32, 40, 56, 57, 58, 59–61, 62, 65, 67, 69, 74, 77, 79, 84, 91, 94–95, 97, 101, 117, 118, 119, 156, 163, 164, 165
  alliance with, 75
  bad, 130
  body, 103
  breast, 103
  creative, 120
  Edward's, 98, 99
  face, 103
  Hamlet's, xiii
  masculine, 63
  once removed, 121
  one step removed, 102

protecting, 96
stranger, 63
transitional, 70, 73, 80, 96, 130, 162, 166
two, 14
as underlying continuing presence, 102
motherhood, 120, 165
motif, dominant, 137
motivation(s), 73, 156, 157
motives, personal, topical, universal, 30
mournfulness, 62
mourning, xv, 134, 161
movements
  body, 36
  dissident, 18
  psychoanalytic, 18
mover, prime, 160
movies, 66, 70
Mozart, W. A., 88, 124
  Leopold, father, 124
  son, Carl, 88
Munter, G., 128
murder, Hamlet's father's, xiii
Murray, L., 173
Murray, P., 173
Muse, 33, 89, 90, 97, 117, 118
museum, 130, 163
Museum of the Duomo, Florence, 15
music, 23, 44, 56–59, 62, 64, 70–71, 104, 129, 133
  nasal, 145
musicality, 72
musician(s), 56, 70, 105
  rock, 57, 69, 79, 80
My Space, 149, *150*
mysteries, 99
mystic, 105
mysticism, 93
myth(s), 42, 100
mythology, 98, 111

name(s), 146
  vile, 78
narrative(s), 5, 28, 33, 41, 42, 43, 44, 53–54, 76, 106

Nash, S., 49, 170
National Gallery, London, 10, 13
Navarre, Marguerite de, 126
negation, 94
negatives, photographic, 24
neurosis, 81, 124
Nevelson, L., 42
New York, 47
  Stock Exchange, 155
newnesses, 43, 97
night, 138
  volunteer, 76
nightmare, 44
Nijinsky, V., xvi
nobility, 128
nobleman, 96, 155
nonactor(s), 136–137
nonself, 91, 92
  personal and impersonal, 107
novel(s), 126–127
Noy, P., 44, 170
Nude Descending a Staircase, A, 41
nurse, wet, 14
nurture, 124

O., Anna. *See Studies on Hysteria*
object, 105, 164, 166
  art, 4, 18, 33, 35, 51, 64, 83, 85, 86, 91, 92, 101, 107, 111, 117, 125
  created, xiii, 23, 32, 51, 103, 134
  cultural, 30, 32, 94
  external, 107
  internal-external mediating, 55
  new, 49, 106, 117, 121
  primary, 120
  religious, 92
  transitional, 32, 55, 63, 90–91, 121
  See also object
object (in psychoanalytic sense), 55, 83–97, 101, 125, 144, 161
  ameliorating, 96
  art as, 86
  dedifferentiation of self and, 98
  dialectical creation of self and, 85
  different order of, 87

differentiated, 165
expanded order of, 89
greater panoply, 87
identificatory, 162
internal–external, 94–95
interpersonal, 87
merger, 105
primal, 105–106, 117
relationships of the creative person, 86
transference, 166
transitional, 91–93, 96, 103
See also object
objectivity, 69, 157
objectlessness, 96, 99
observation, infant, 85
oeuvre, of the artist, 117
officialdom, 141, 160
O'Keeffe, G., 129
Olivier, L., 155
Olympia Apollo, 41
omnipotence, 163
    creative, 114
    magical-hallucinatory, 31
oneness
    primal, 111
    safe, 96
onslaught, 78
ontogenesis, 31, 51, 86, 103, 107, 114
ontogeny, xii, 55, 85
opposite, turning to the, 53
opposition, 46–47
optics, laser, 154
opus, 156
ordeal, timeless, 59
Oremland, J. D., xiv, xvi, 6, 42, 44, 50, 51,
        53, 55, 65, 80, 81, 106, 123–126,
        128–130, 131–134, 137, 138, 139–
        140, 141, 142, 144–145, 146–147,
        149, 151, 154, 157, 159–160, 168,
        170
orientation, dyadic material, 120
origin(s), 62, 89, 90
    creativity, 51, 52, 107
original, 93, 96, 161
originality, 55, 83, 99, 100, 127, 161, 162

in creativity, 86
Origins and Psychodynamics of Creativ-
        ity, The, 131
Ostwald, P., xvi, 171
other, 32, 40, 79, 103, 162
    differentiated sense of, 131
    impersonal, 55
    internalized primal, 91
    interpersonal, 55, 85
    primal, 93, 96
outcast, fear of, 129
overawareness, 161
overvaluing, commercial, 161
overview, 157

package, financial, 154
Packard, D., 159
painter(s), 73, 83, 91, 96, 123, 125, 128,
        132, 134, 154, 160–163, 165–166
    abstract, 34
painting(s), 23, 37, 91, 94, 97, 104, 109,
        147
    Spanish Catholic religious, 42
palette, 149
Panofsky, E., 5–9, 100, 171
pantheon, creative, 145
papacy, Roman, 41
paradigm(s)
    art, 41
    psychoanalytic, 51
parameters, new, 141
paranoia, 68, 133
parent(s), 134, 156, 161
parody, 76
parsimony, 43, 137
    principle of, 22, 25
part self and part other, 125
participant, provoking, 67
participation, indirect, 159
particularity, 94
part-me and part-not-me, 90
partner(s), 72, 80
    founding, 151
partnership, 152
parturition, 118

passion(s), 131, 145
  human, 128
passive to active, 80
past, 117
  unconscious, 102
paternity, burden of, 129
pathography, xv, xvi, 4
patina, rust-red, 45
patron, 41, 46, 80, 86, 95–101, 118, 128,
    130, 156, 159, 166
  as intrapsychic concept, 95, 96
  as person, 95, 97
  male and female, 163
  modern day, 162
peers, 78
pen names, masculine, 127
penis, 58, 60, 120
perfection, 158, 162, 163
performance, codified, 138
performers, 53, 56, 79, 80, 102, 139
perils, 146
  to creativity, 117–118
period
  adolescent fat, 57, 61
  rehearsal, 161
  transitional, 105
Perkins, F., 104
Perkins, T., 151
Perloff, C., 131
perpetuators, 92
perpetuity, personal, 117
perserverance, 78
persistence, 77
person(s), 84, 85, 106, 161
personality, 55, 73, 90, 95, 156, 158
perversion, 110
phallus, 63
phase
  tertiary, 161
  transitional 90–91, 95, 101, 107, 164
phenomena, 63
  transitional, 92
phobia, 71
physicist, 97
physics, 99

Piaget, J., 54, 171
Picasso, P., 43, 97, 118, 124, 125
pietá(s), 14
  Florentine, 14, *15*
  Saint Peter's, 14, *17*, 41
  Rondanini, 14, *19*
Pinocoteca Comunale-Faenza, 7
Pinter, H., 137–138, 162
Pisan, Christine de, 126
pity, 87, 117
plan, game, 157
plate, 147
platform, free-floating, 137
play, 30, 36, 54–55, 66, 69, 70, 90, 99,
    132, 133, 134, 135, 136, 137, 138,
    139, 140, 147, 155, 157, 160, 161,
    162, 163, 164
  child's, 102
  one-act, 67
playing, 54–55, 72, 73, 153, 161
  art of, 138
playlets, 132, 163
playwright, 70
pleasure, 54, 159
poem, 126, 149
poet(s), 90, 97, 117, 123, 126, 132
poetry, 23, 87, 90, 97
polarities, 147
polarizations, 118
Pollock, G., 44, 171, 172
Pollock, J., 96
Pollock, S., 97
Polydorus, 135
Polymestor, 136
pope, 96
Popova, L., 128
Portal Series I, 147, *148*
portraiture, Roman, 141
Poskitt, J., 89, 171
potency, father's, 117
potter, 88
power, 76, 161
  emotional, 40
  evocative, 9, 39, 40
  over the father, 57

practice, 151
Praxiteles, 41
pregnancy, 118
preoccupation(s)
    autistic, 100
    father's, 120
presence
    inner, 28
    protective, 93
presences, external, 90, 103
Pride and Prejudice, 127
priest, 95
primacy, 41
prince, 96
Princesse de Clèves, La, 127
principals, 145
principle
    fundamental, 54
    organizing, 39
print, Galton, 24
Prize, Nobel, 97
problems, sexual, 99
process(es), 85
    artistic, 141, 160
    creating(ive), xvi, 49, 53, 142, 151, 157
    differentiated tertiary, 105
    directing, 155
    interpersonal, 50
    intuitive, 105
    psychical transforming, 94
    psychophysiological, 84
    rehearsal, 132–134, 163
    transformational, 95
    unconscious mental, 110
proclivity, 145
procreation(ing), 117, 121, 165
producer, film, 154
product, 133–134, 155, 160
profession, 62, 73
profile, classic, 72
profitability, 153–154
program
    sculpture, 144
    special for gifted children, 99
progression(s), 64, 146

linear, 161
    recapitulated, 105
prohibitions, 147
project, 166
    ceiling, 101
    science, 98
    superhuman, 101
projections, 27, 36, 84
propaganda, 42
property of the mind, 54
proscenium, 137
prose, 127
Prosser, E., xiv, 171
Proust, M., 124
Providence, psychoanalytically oriented, 106
provocation, 67
psyche, 145
psychiatrist, 100
psychoanalysis, 165, 166
psychoanalyst, 166, 123
psychodynamics, 21, 39, 58, 71
    of talent, 53, 56
psychogenetics, 21
psychologist, 73
psychology, analytical, 6,
psychopathology, xiv, xvi, 3–4, 110, 123
psychosis, 68
psychotic, 99
puberty, 57, 61
publishers, 127
punishment(s), 61, 62

quality
    comedic, 79
    exceptional, 80
    kinesthetic, 103
    redemptive, 144
quartet, 62, 71
quest, artist's, 125

rage, 18, 39, 61
    impotent, 67
randomness, 158
Rauschenberg, R., 147

reaffirmation, actualized, 96
reality, 86, 138, 158–159, 163
 construction of, 31
 intrapsychic, 93
 social, 93–94
realm, interpersonal, 106
rebels, antisocial, 129
recapitulation(s), 24
 developmental, 64
 ontogenetic, 64, 161
recitation, dead, 132
recitative, 145, 164
recreation, 80
rediscovery, 43
reductionism, 4, 37
redundancy, 43, 137
reemergence, 80
reenactment
 masochistic, 70
 organized, 79
refuelling, 104
regression, 31, 98
rehearsal(s), 69, 131–132, 133, 137
Reifenstahl, L., 42
reincarnation, 130, 166
reinternalizations, 84
Reiser, M., 44, 171
relatedness, xii, 32, 92
 heterosexual interpersonal, 118
 interpersonal, 85, 87, 106
 object, 51, 53, 81, 90, 93, 100, 106,
  110, 117, 144, 161
relationship(s), 62, 65, 74, 80, 89, 98,
  145, 163
 of the artist to art, 90, 107
 father-son, 101
 Fliess–Freud, 99
 formal, 18
 interpersonal, 90
 object, 87
 patron-artist, 100
 personal, 86
 primal, 165
 transitional, 166
relativity, 158

religion(s), 92–93
reminiscences, 88
remorse, 119
Renaissance, 96
repetition, 39, 56, 149
replenishment, 90, 106
replications, multiple, 162
representation(s), 63, 94
 external, institutionalized, 121
 external, multilevel communicating, 95
 means of, 22
 mythic, 89
 object, 84, 91
 self, 91
 unconscious, 33
 visual, 18
repressed, return of, 1, 26
repression, 124
reprobates, unredeemable, 129
reprojections, 84
requirements, internal and external, 161
Research and Development Limited Partnerships, 153
residue, day, 23, 29–30
resistance, 36
respondents, xii, 160–161, 163, 165, 166
responses, 123–166
restructurings, financial, 162
resurrection, 41
 primal, 14
retaliation, 71, 80
reunion
 primal, 42
 regressive, 63
 safe, 80
revelations, 100, 145
revenue, 153–154
revision, secondary, 23, 28
rewards, financial, 159
rhythm, 104, 139
Richard III, 42, 155–156
Richards, A. D., 171, 172
Richards, A. K., 171, 172
Richardson, J., 97, 118, 171
Richelieu, Cardinal, 127

Ricoeur, P., 93, 94, 171
ritual(s), 145, 164
rock, 56–58, 62
Rodin, A., 48
role(s), 69, 70, 80
  comedic, 65
romanticism, 91
Rome, 41, 141
Roosevelt, F. D., 104–105
Rorschach Projection Test, 27
Rosanova, 128
Rose, G., xvi, 53, 65, 81, 171
Rosekrans, J. N., 44–46
Rothschilds, the, 124
Rousseau, J., 129
routine(s), 76, 80
  formalized, 128
Ruben, P., 42
rules, 30, 157
Ryle, M., 167

Sacks, C., 168
Sacrifice of Noah, 111, *115*
St. Anne, 10
St. Anne and Two Others, 10, *11,* 14
St. John, 9, *10,* 114
St. Mary, 10, 14
St. Peter, 5
sales, product, 153
salesman, traveling, 57, 74
Salomé, 7–8
San Francisco Chronicle, 47
San Francisco Museum of Modern Art,
  47–48
San Pietro in Vincoli, 18, 20
Sand, G., 127
Sappho, 126
satiation, 84
Satie, E., 156
satisfaction, 84
satisfiers, external, 84
Savage, D., 171
saw, band, 145, 146
scaffolding, flimsy, 149
Scaffolding Series I, 149, *152*

scenery, 136
Schapiro, M., xiv, 9, 14, 22, 171
schemes, 37
Schiele, E., 96
  Schiele's Wally, 96
scholars
  art, historical, 100
  Michelangelo, 111
  psychoanalytic, 100
school, 78, 79
  acting, 76
  high, 76
Schultz, C., 32
Schumann, R., xvi
science, 30, 124, 153, 155
scientists, 43, 83, 159
  mad, 98
scope, 156, 157, 159
score, 70
screen
  cinema, 30, 102
  dream, 32, 102, 103
script(s), 69, 155
sculptor(s), 83, 91, 129, 140, 142,
  145–147, 154, 160–162, 164, 165
  minimalist metal, 44
sculpture(s), 23, 44, 45, 47, 91, 109,
  144–146, 149, 160
  Hindu, 42
  perfect, 141
  Spanish Catholic religious, 42
Sculpture Park, Roseville, California, 143
search, artistic, 165
Securities and Exchange Commission,
  153
seduction
  Hamlet's mother, xiii
  homosexual, 75–76, 79
self, xii, 32, 39, 44, 49, 50, 85, 91, 92,
  103, 105, 107, 117, 165
  dedifferentiation of, 98
  differentiated sense of, 131
  inner, 125
  primal, 114
self-absorption, 105

self-assurance, 157
self-centered, 87
self-conception, parthenogenic, 111
self-confidence, 74, 125, 157, 158
self-definition, 84
self-derision, 74
self-doubt, 158
self-emasculation, 61
self-enhancement, 50
self-examination, 157
self-expression, 85
self-fellatio, 111
self-insemination, oral, 111
self-integration, 92
self-realization, 106
self-representation, 64
self-restraint, 129
self-transcendence, 50, 85, 87
self-valildation, 50, 84, 85, 87, 106
self-verification, 85, 87
seminology, 5
sense, subjective
   intuitive, 137
   of shifting maleness and femaleness,
      107
   of shifting masculinity and feminin-
      ity, 111
sensitivity, heightened, 52
separateness, 64
separation, 32, 39, 80
   fusion-separation, 64
Separation of Light from Darkness, 111,
   114
Series, Portal, *See Portal Series I*
Serra, R., 44, 46, 47, 48, 144
set, 66, 67, 72, 137–138
Settignano, 14
sex(es), 74, 121, 127
   physicality of, 42
   same, 110
sexualilty, infantile, 2
Shakespeare, W., xiii–xv, 42, 43, 172
   father, xiv
   son, Hamnet, xiv–xv
shape(s), 85, 147

curvilinear, 142
Sharpe, E. F., 23, 172
shelter, 136
   homeless, 48
Sherwood, R., 104
shifting passive to active, 54
Shiva. *See Ardhanarisvara*
signature(s), 146
   semiological, 5
Silas Marner, 127
Silva, V. da, 129
Sinding-Larsen, S., 37, 172
Sistine Chapel Ceiling, 41, 43
   decoration of, 101
   Histories, 111
skill(s), 52, 124, 151
   people, 156
skit(s), 76, 78–79
sleep, 31, 123, 140
slips, 33
smile, 75
   characteristic (Leonardo), 9
Smoke-Enders, 74
Snyder, F., 31, 172
society, 121, 129
software, 159
solace, 76
soloist, 71
solution(s), 157, 158, 163
   creative, 137
son, 124, 135, 140
songs, 146
sonnents, 126
sonography, computed, 155
Soper, K., 167
soul, 145
sound(s), 85, 87, 103, 140
   haunting, 135
source, ultimate, 111
space(s), 64, 72, 73, 133, 137
   negative, 147, 149
   public, 141, 146
   transitional, 90–91
spark, creative, 139
speech, collective, 135

spheres, 41
spinoffs, 162
spouse(s), 61, 165
stability, 40, 84
stage, 66, 67, 69, 136, 137, 138, 139
stalemate, 166
Standard Edition, 18
Stanford University, 140
star
    provocative, 59
    rock, 56
Stassinopoulos, A., 118, 172
state
    design, 141, 160
    mystical, 105
    trance-like, 149
statues, gigantic, 141
steel, Corten, 44
Stein, G., 127
Steinberg, L., xiv, 172
Steinman, E., 18, 172
Stern, D. N., 85, 172
Stinson, H., 105
Storey, D., 133
Streetcar Named Desire, A, 43
Strindberg, A., 145, 172
stroke, master, 156
structure, 154
    of the art object, 107
    autoerotic, 111
    character, 69
    financial, 153
    hermaphroditic, 111
    new, 153
    safe, 149
structuring, intrapsychic, 110
struggles, 76
students, 68
    dissident, 67
Studies on Hysteria, 2
studio, 132, 142, 144–145, 149
style, 53–54, 94, 126, 160
    artistic, 51
    dress, 58
sublimation, 55, 86, 93–95

affinity to creativity, 81
    object-related view of, 94
"Sublimation: A Frontier Concept," 30
substance, 111
substitution, 139
subterfuge, brilliant, 133
success, 156, 160
suicide, 77, 118
superego, 94
suppression, 124
sword, 6–8
symbol(s), 27, 32, 44
    classical, 5
    ever-varying, 92
    new, 24
    novel, 107
symbolization, 91
symmetry, 39, 40, 103, 147
sympathy, 126
symptom(s), 33, 43, 71, 79
    hysterical, 3–4
    physical, 1
synergism, seamless, 43
synthesis, 55
    magical, 95
systems
    developmental, 85
    value, 142

Taj Mahal, 42
talent, xi, 51–53, 55, 57, 62–63, 64, 69,
    70, 73, 75, 76, 78, 80, 96, 124,
    144, 153, 156, 165
    and psychoanalysis, 81
    as a defense against being creative,
        56, 151
    relation of creativity and, 79, 141
talentum (Latin), 51
talisman, 71
Tanning, D., 129
task
    artistic, 141
    impossible, 100
    simple, 137
teacher, 56, 75, 99, 130, 131

technique(s), 138, 161
Post-Stanislavskian, 139
technology, 155, 157, 159
Tekla, 145
television, 73, 77
Tempest, The, 43
template, 103
tension
drive, 83–84
dynamic, 48
terms
interpersonal, 91
ontogenetic, 95
terror, 69, 87, 117, 140
Testament, 7, 8, 111
text, 70, 133
that, the, 55, 85, 86, 93, 107
theater, 67, 109, 134, 137
theme(s), 39, 42, 78, 103, 107
central, 22
homoerotic, 111
psychoanalytic study of, 86
unitary, 37
theory(ies), 158
drive, 83
scientific, 94
weak, 118
thing(s), 92, 164
connotative, 85, 90, 91
depersonalized, 83
inanimate, 32
sweet young, 67
Thinker, The, 48
thinking, creative, 104
Thomas, D., 87, 88, 172
thought, 160
collective, 135
discursive, 28
formation of, 84
Tiepolos, the, 124
Tilted Arc, 47
timeless, 160
title, 28, 146
''To Whom Does One Relate One's
Dreams?,'' 25

Tolnay, C. de, xiv, 100, 172
tour(s), 59, 72
tower, clock, 146
tragedy, Greek, 135
training, 128, 151
actor, 138
trait(s), 1, 24, 33, 54, 78, 109
transference, 166
transformations, 93–95
trauma, 39, 107
trial and error, 54
trials, clinical, 153
triangulation, oedipal, xiii
Trietler, L., 43, 172
Triumph of the Will, The, 42
trombone, 57–60, 62
tunes, 61, 63–64
turnings, spatial, 54
twitches, body and facial, 75
typology, 25
typus christi, 25

Ulrich, A., 172
uncle, Hamlet's, xiii
Uncle Vanya, 131
unconscious, 2, 126, 163
unconventionality, 129
understanding, 3, 33, 37, 151, 156, 158
clairvoyant, 105
meta-iconographic, 8
union, 63, 90, 105
unity, primal, 114
universals, 4, 39, 149
developmental, xii
human, xiv, xvi
understanding of, 3
university, 67–68, 96, 98–99, 130
unpleasure, 84
un-self consciousness, 138, 161

Valadon, S., 128
values, psychical, 94–95
Vasari, G., 96
Vatican, Monumenti Musei e Gallerie
Pontificie, 114–116

venture(s), 153, 154
Vere, E. de (Earl of Oxford), xv
verification, search for, 90
victim, 67, 78
view, 158, 163
    hereditary, 53
    schematic, 102
viewer, 16, 35, 38, 39, 44, 45, 101, 142
Vigée-Lebrun, E., 128
Vinci, L. da, xv, 9–14, 16, 114
    life and art of, 110
    worship of Salai (''Little Satan''), 110
violin, 120
violinist, 56, 70–71, 79, 80, 120
virtuoso, cello, 88
vista, 142, 157, 164
visualization, 31
vocabulary, 23, 149
vocation, 128
voice(s), 52, 76, 77, 138, 146
void, 60, 63
vulnerability, 78

waiter, 73, 76, 78, 79
wakefulness, 123
waking, 158
wall, Sistine Chapel, 111
Wallace, W., 169
war, armature, 141
War, Secretary of, 105
watch, gold pocket, 71, 72
Webster, P. D., xiv, 172
wellspring(s), 157
    unconscious, 151
Whan, E., 168
Wharton, E., 127
White Memorial Fountain, 140
Whitebook, J., 30, 93, 94, 172
who, a, 93
wife(ves), 14, 118, 121, 146, 165
Wilson, L., xvi, 42, 172
windows, stained glass, 128
Winnicott, D. W., 31–32, 55, 81, 90–92,
        106, 172
wisdom, 106
wish(es), 1, 31

high-level, ethereal, 84
oedipal, 3
to look, 2
witness, 62, 163
Wohl, A. S., 167
Wölfflin, H., 18, 173
woman (women), 8, 13, 65, 89–90,
        126–130, 136, 147, 162, 163
    children of, 119
    creative, 117–120, 139, 165
    displaced, 135
    domestic, 97, 117
    entwined, 12
    gifted, 129
    neighbor, 60
    other, 117
    particular kind of, 96
    professional, 130
    Trojan, 135
    work of, 119
wonder, 87
wood, 145, 146
Woolf, V., 127
Word, the, 92
words, 87
work, 77, 106, 157, 161
    commissioned, 146
    hackneyed, 132
workshop, 136
world, 95, 127, 135, 140, 141, 160
    business, 157, 159, 162
    dream, 149, 158, 163
    internal and external, 90, 107
    interpersonal, 86
    love affair with, 87
    new, 96
    observable, 111
    visual, 132, 136
worship, pagan, 18
writers, 43, 83, 123, 166
writing, 109
    psychoanalytic, 165
Wuthering Heights, 127
Wysuph, C. L., 97, 173

Yourcenar, M., 127

Zelazo, P. R., 85, 169